FOUNDATION —4— MARRIAGE

THE FOUR GIFTS OF LOVE® LIFESTYLE

DR. JENNIFER HARLEY CHALMERS
DR. WILLARD F. HARLEY, JR.

Foundation 4 Marriage: The Four Gifts of Love® Lifestyle
Copyright © 2023 by Marriage Resources International, Inc., and Jennifer Harley Chalmers. All rights reserved.

The core of this book was previously published under *The Four Gifts of Love® Participant's Guide: Revised and Expanded Edition for the Four Gifts of Love® Class*, Copyright © 2004, 2016, by Jennifer H. Chalmers and Willard F. Harley, Jr. ISBN 978-0-692-06097-1

The Gift of Care Logo, Gift of Protection Logo, Gift of Honesty Logo, and Gift of Time Logo. Copyright © 2016 by Jennifer H. Chalmers. All rights reserved.

Four Gifts of Love® is a registered trademark and cannot be used without permission from the authors.

For more information about the Four Gifts of Love® lifestyle, please visit:
https://www.Foundation4Marriage.COM
https://www.FourGiftsofLove.Org

Unless otherwise indicated, all Scripture quotations are from the ESV® Bible (The Holy Bible, English Standard Version®), copyright © 2001 by Crossway, a publishing ministry of Good News Publishers. Used by permission. All rights reserved.

Scripture quotations labeled NIV are taken from the Holy Bible: New International Version®. Copyright © 1973, 1978, 1984, 2011 by Biblica, Inc.® All rights reserved worldwide. Used by permission of Zondervan Bible Publishers.

Scripture quotations labeled NLT are from the *Holy Bible,* New Living Translation, copyright © 1996, 2004, 2015 by Tyndale House Foundation. Used by permission of Tyndale House Publishers Inc., Carol Stream, Illinois 60188. All rights reserved.

Original photography by A. Chalmers-Grosz. Used by permission.

Published by Marriage Resources International, Inc.

Cover design by Jennifer H. Chalmers

ISBN-13: 979-8-218-19557-1

CONTENTS

1

The Four Gifts of Love:
A Solid Foundation

You are about to read about a lifestyle designed to create a solid foundation for your marriage by giving and receiving the Four Gifts of Love. While it's about giving and receiving these gifts in marriage, it's also about giving and receiving the Four Gifts of Love in your relationship with God.

Before I introduce the Four Gifts of Love, let me explain why both of these important relationships will be considered in this book. (And, we, Drs. Chalmers and Harley will use "I" to refer to either of us as we describe our experience and counsel.)

Which relationships will affect you the most in your lifetime? As a psychologist, I've had many opportunities to hear the intimate details of people's lives, and one important detail I've heard is the way people are affected by their relationships. My clients have described problems with their boss at work, with parents, neighbors, friends, grandparents, and children. I've also heard how fulfilling these relationships can be when they're on track.

> Which relationships will affect you the most in your lifetime?

Of all the relationships my clients describe, the one they consistently identify as best when going well and worst when going badly is their marital relationship. It can be a primary source of happiness and satisfaction, or it can be a primary source of unhappiness and frustration.

Your marital relationship will have a greater effect on your life than any other human relationship. So for that reason, I want you to learn how to have a marriage that's consistently a primary source of happiness and fulfillment for both you and your spouse.

But there is another relationship that has an even greater impact on our lives—now and forever. It's our relationship with God. Unlike human relationships, this one impacts everything we are and will be.

To God, you are priceless, wondrously created, earnestly and persistently sought after, and abundantly loved. You are not an accident of nature but someone created to be valuable to God. And when you enter into a relationship with Him, Jesus said, "there is joy before the angels of God" (Luke 15:10). What other relationship can compare to our relationship with Him?

These two, personal, bilateral, long-term relationships—with your spouse and with God—will affect you more than anything else in life. And since they're so important, it makes sense to do whatever you can to make them both TERRIFIC at the same time!

But that's not the only reason to make these two relationships terrific. Jesus Christ said in Matthew 22: 37-40 (NIV), "'Love the Lord your God with all your heart and with all your soul and with all your mind.' This is the first and greatest commandment. And the second is like it: 'Love your neighbor as yourself.' All the Law and the Prophets hang on these two commandments." God wants our complete devotion—heart, soul, and mind. But He doesn't stop there.

He also wants our care for others to reflect the love we have for Him and reflect how we want to be treated ourselves. And who is your closest neighbor? Who can you truly love more than any other person on earth? It's your spouse.

The Four Gifts of Love that you will be studying in these chapters have already helped millions throughout the world develop wonderful marriages—sustaining the feeling of love for a lifetime. But these same gifts can also be applied to developing a more intimate and devoted relationship with God. By following the concepts within these chapters, you will be creating a lifestyle that allows both of these important and unique relationships to flourish.

Although this material was first intended to help marriages, many engaged couples have found it helpful to prepare their marriage with a solid foundation. So, this book will often use the term *partner* in reference to *fiancée/fiancé* or *spouse*.

Let me introduce the Four Gifts of Love.

- The gift of Care is a *willingness* and *effort* to do what you can to make the other happy. It puts your desire to do meaningful acts of care into daily action—*being a primary source of happiness.*

  Mary looks forward to her husband, Dennis, calling her during his lunch break at work. He wants to know how her day is going and it proves to her that she's in his thoughts. She is equally interested in Dennis's day and his accomplishments. He feels appreciated and admired by her words of encouragement and thanks. Those daily calls are one of the ways Dennis and Mary give each other the gift of care.

  Every couple makes a promise to care for each other at the altar, but few understand what it means. You will have an advantage over most couples because you will learn how to care and intentionally practice your caring skills. In marriage, you will learn that the gift of Care = meeting emotional needs.

You will also learn something else that's even more important—your care for each other is one of the ways you can give God the gift of care. He is pleased when we obey His commands, and as we have just read in Matthew 22, one of His commands is that we care for our partner as we want to be cared for.

In Part One, you will learn about meaningful ways that partners can care for each other. You will also review meaningful ways to please God. With that information, you will have an opportunity to apply your knowledge by actually creating a lifestyle that gives this gift—being a primary source of happiness within these two relationships.

- The gift of Protection is a *willingness* and *effort* to do what you can to avoid making the other unhappy—*to avoid being a source of unhappiness.*

Jon is asked by his friends to join a basketball team. But before making the decision, he asks Kathy, his wife, how she would feel about the idea. They both know that decisions made without a mutually enthusiastic agreement could hurt one of them. By considering each other's feelings before they act, they are protecting each other from their own selfishness. This is one way they give the gift of protection.

And Jon and Kathy protect in other ways. They avoid selfish demands, disrespectful judgments, dishonesty, angry outbursts, independent behavior, and annoying habits (these behaviors are called "Love Busters"). They understand that the gift of protection is not about protecting each other from the world; it's about protecting each other from their own Love Busters. In marriage, the gift of Protection = no Love Busters.

In Part One, you and your spouse will be learning how to be a source of each other's happiness and God's pleasure. But unless you do something to prevent it, you can also become a source of great sadness. That's why this gift is equally important. Part Two will help you identify behaviors that bring unhappiness to your partner and God. You will also learn how to avoid those behaviors in both relationships.

- The gift of Honesty is a *willingness* and *effort* to do what you can to make *everything* about yourself transparent to the other—what you've done in the past, what you're doing in the present, and what you plan to do in the future.

Whenever Myrna and Ronald have breakfast, they review their plans for the day—where they can be reached, meetings they've scheduled and with whom, the time they will be arriving home, and thoughts for evening or weekend plans. They also keep each other informed if plans change. This is one way they give each other the gift of honesty.

Being honest in marriage requires complete honesty about your feelings, your personal history, your current activities and experiences, and your future plans. Without this gift, the necessary adjustments to each other won't be made— you won't be able to find mutually acceptable solutions to problems. Without honesty, you won't know how to give the gifts of care and protection effectively. In other words, the gift of Honesty = transparency.

God also wants your gift of honesty. Granted, He already knows everything there is to know about you. Yet, He still wants you to tell Him about your plans, feelings, and thoughts—regularly communicating your understanding of Him and yourself.

Part Three will review this gift and help you give the gift of honesty to your partner and God.

- The gift of **Time** is a *willingness* and *effort* to give undivided attention, using the time to provide the most meaningful acts of care for the other.

Sherry and Joe have an appointment with each other every Sunday afternoon at 3:30. That's when they schedule time for the upcoming week to meet each other's most intimate emotional needs. It's the way they give each other the gift of time.

This gift is an important ingredient for any long-term relationship, but it's essential for those who promise to give the gifts of care, protection, and honesty. Without the gift of time, you cannot effectively give and receive the other gifts. In other words, the gift of Time = undivided attention doing meaningful acts of care.

Part Four will review this gift and help you give the gift of time to your partner and God.

A commitment to creating a solid foundation with the Four Gifts of Love as a lifestyle, a focus on your two most important relationships, and the willingness and effort that reflects your commitment within these relationships—that's what this book is about.

And when you are done reading this book, we recommend that you consider taking the Four Gifts of Love® Class. This eight-lesson class offers a review of the readings within this book but also provides professionally-animated review videos, more in-depth guided assignments,  questionnaires, and much more. This class provides a bridge from knowledge to a Four Gifts of Love® lifestyle. Please visit https://www.FourGiftsofLove.Org for more information about starting your first lesson for free, or scan the QR code.

⚙ *Talk About This*

This is your first Talk About This with your partner. Please keep the conversation **BRIEF** and **STAY ON** the topic of the questions. And most importantly, use this time to practice your gifts of care and protection, being especially careful to avoid disrespectful comments. Remember, your goals are to be a source of happiness and avoid being a source of pain in your relationship.

1. Review: What are the Four Gifts of Love? (the four categories and definitions)

2. Who and what are affected by your marriage relationship? Try to come up with at least 20. (See below if you would like some help.)

3. Discuss the truth of this statement: Your relationship with your spouse is the most important human relationship you will ever have. Why?

4. Who and what are affected by a relationship with God? (See below if you would like some help.)

5. Do YOU expect that YOU will be able to perfectly implement the new ideas and habits immediately and perfectly? The answer is probably "no." Why? An unintended but instinctual attitude when starting this book is that it may raise your expectations for your partner's changes. The expectation could be for your partner to be a "superpartner" and perfectly learn the new habits. Because we all know it takes time and practice to learn new habits and make lifestyle changes.

> "What can I do to make this relationship better?"

6. Right now, agree with your partner to focus on your own changes (i.e., self-change) since that is all you have control over, and write down this phrase somewhere (e.g., sticky note, piece of paper) so you can see it clearly: "What can I do to make this relationship better?" Agreed?

(Did you come up with these for question #2? physical health, finances, children, extended family, family, values, ministry, testimony, career choice, job performance, education, emotions, self-esteem, mental health, community, diet, vacations, parenting skills, hobbies, retirement, budget, weight, view of marriage, stress level, hygiene, society, social skills, rules of life, goals, self-discipline, laws, energy, decisions, priorities, world view, economy, relationship with God, and legacy!)

(Did you come up with these for question #4? Copy everything from the list above, but there is SO much more ... eternal life, salvation, view of other's worth, self-worth, view of forgiveness, meaning of life, spiritual comfort in times of trouble, marriage, commitment, obedience to God's teaching)

2

The Four Gifts of Love with God ...
The Amazing Effect

✝

Τhe Bible provides many examples of what happens to those who put these gifts of love into action with God. I've chosen a familiar story to demonstrate this amazing effect.

This is the story of Zacchaeus from Luke 19:1-10. These verses describe a relationship between Zacchaeus and God—through the Son, Jesus Christ. As you read, imagine yourself being there. Imagine the feelings of Jesus, the crowd, and especially Zacchaeus. Look for the specific and meaningful acts that demonstrate gifts of love within this relationship and their effect on Zacchaeus.

¹ He [Jesus] entered Jericho and was passing through.

> ➤ *His journey to Jerusalem had already been delayed when He had healed two blind men just outside of Jericho. His journey was about to be interrupted again.*

² And behold, there was a man named Zacchaeus. He was a chief tax collector and was rich.

> ➤ *Zacchaeus was a Jew who was excluded and hated by the Jewish people because he collected taxes for the Roman government, and occasionally overcharged, keeping the difference for himself.*

³ And he was seeking to see who Jesus was,

> *Word had spread about the miracles of Jesus, and He drew quite a crowd whenever people recognized Him. The healing of the two blind men outside Jericho had probably increased those numbers substantially. He was a celebrity, and people in all walks of life wanted to see Him.*

but on account of the crowd, he could not because he was small in stature. [4] So he ran on ahead and climbed up into a sycamore tree to see him, for he was about to pass that way.

> *Jesus was probably walking slowly enough along a well-traveled road that Zacchaeus could anticipate where He was headed and thought the leaves of the tree would hide him.*

[5] And when Jesus came to the place, he looked up and said to him, "Zacchaeus, hurry and come down, for I must stay at your house today."

> *Jesus was direct and powerful. He knew Zacchaeus was in the tree and even knew him by name. He also knew that Zacchaeus needed something only He could give—a relationship with God that would transform his life. Yet, even though Jesus' words were strong, He didn't make Zacchaeus accept His invitation. Zacchaeus had to make a choice.*

[6] So he hurried and came down and received him joyfully.

> *Zacchaeus could have refused the generous offer made by Jesus. Instead, he enthusiastically welcomed Jesus and accepted His invitation.*

[7] And when they saw it, they all grumbled, "He has gone to be the guest of a man who is a sinner."

➤ *Zacchaeus was very unpopular because he cheated so many people. So the people in Jericho didn't think he deserved Christ's invitation.*

[8] And Zacchaeus stood and said to the Lord, "Behold, Lord, the half of my goods I give to the poor. And if I have defrauded anyone of anything, I restore it fourfold."

➤ *Jesus and Zacchaeus may have spent time sitting and talking together. We don't know exactly what happened, but we know the result—Zacchaeus's perspective on life had radically changed.*

➤ *Zacchaeus was once a lover of money, a cheater, a traitor, and a man who was separated from God and hated by many. Yet, after Zacchaeus accepted Jesus as the Lord and spent time with Him, his values changed. He became passionate about becoming honest and a lover of people, having a restored relationship with God and others. From that day forward, he saw things differently.*

[9] And Jesus said to him, "Today salvation has come to this house, since he also is a son of Abraham. [10] For the Son of Man came to seek and to save the lost."

➤ *Jesus makes a point that He repeats throughout His ministry: He came to save us from a life separated from God. While everyone is "lost" because of their thoughtlessness, sometimes those regarded as most thoughtless are the most willing to turn away from a life that is separated from God to receive His gift of eternal life through faith in Jesus Christ.*

What an amazing day for Zacchaeus! He accepted Jesus' invitation to enter into a relationship with Him. That relationship with Christ also inspired Zacchaeus to live a life pleasing to God. His perspective on life was changed and a passion for pleasing his Lord was created.

> That relationship with Christ inspires us to live a life pleasing to God.

Giving the Four Gifts of Love means *doing* actions that are specific and meaningful: Actions that give the gifts of care, protection, honesty, and time. The effect of entering into a relationship with Him through faith, then giving and receiving these gifts with God, is life-transforming; there is a changed perspective on what's important and a new passion for pleasing Him.

Thought Questions

1. Think about your relationship with God. Have you created a lifestyle that continually invites Him into each day? Do you seek to learn more about Him? Do you actively turn away from behaviors that displease Him? Are you honest about what you have done? Do you make lifestyle choices that please God?

2. If the answers to the above questions are "yes," do you notice anything different about your perspective on life as compared to a time in the past when you may not have given God these gifts? Do you notice a greater passion for God? Do you feel closer to Him?

3. If the answers to the above questions are "no," the following chapters will help you create a gift-giving and gift-receiving lifestyle so you can personally feel the incredible effects!

3
A Lifetime of Love

M ary started to unpack the last remaining boxes from their recent move. With a new home, two children, and successful careers, she and her husband, Dennis, were well on their way to having the life they always wanted.

As she sorted through the recipe books, novels, and photo albums from one of the boxes, out came a DVD of their wedding. "How did that get in there?" she asked herself. Curious, she set aside the sorting duty and viewed it, fast-forwarding to when she was coming down the aisle. The sequence of images captured Dennis tearing up as he saw his bride. Mary was also caught with tears of joy as she looked upon her groom. The day had finally arrived. They were to be husband and wife, in love for a lifetime.

At that moment, Mary suddenly and unexpectedly burst into tears. But these were not tears of joy, these were tears of sadness. "How could we have lost something so precious," she thought. They had a house, children, and financial stability, but Mary knew they had lost the "something" that helped inspire them to achieve these life accomplishments together. They lost their love.

As a marriage counselor, I have devoted my life to helping couples turn their marriages from tragic to sensational. Usually, the couples who seek my help have done so much damage to their relationships that it's hard to believe that their marriage could ever be saved. They've failed to provide each other with care, protection, honesty, and time for so long that their love is a distant memory. Yet when they learn to give these gifts to each other, their love will be restored, and their marriage back on solid ground.

What a pity that these couples did not begin their marriage the right way. They thought the love they felt for each other on their wedding day was all they would need. They didn't realize that there are four gifts that are essential for a healthy marriage and that they would lose their love for each other without them. Their dream of a fulfilling marriage became a nightmare because they didn't give each other the Four Gifts of Love.

Care. Protection. Honesty. Time. These are the key gifts I encourage couples to give to each other—and to keep giving for a lifetime. You probably did these things for each other throughout your courtship. It's what people in love do—and it's why you fell in love in the first place. When these four gifts are given, they create and sustain the feeling of love. If you continue to give them, you'll be as much in love throughout your entire marriage as you were on your wedding day. But if you stop—as so many couples do after marriage—your love will be lost and your marriage will be threatened. If you want to experience a lifetime of love together, you need to give the four gifts to each other and then keep giving them throughout your lives.

Love Keeps Marriages Healthy

How did you and your partner decide to marry? Did you discuss the pros and cons of your lifelong marriage with your friends and relatives? Did you take a test to determine if you are compatible? Did you find that you each meet objective criteria that predict marital success?

You may have done some of these things, but even if you did, I doubt that they had much effect on your decision. Most couples marry each other because they are in love and cannot imagine living without each other. They marry because they find each other irresistible.

That's how it was for me and my wife, Joyce. Long before I asked her to marry me, we both knew that we could not possibly be happy without each other. I was in love with her and she with me. We spent part of every day with each other and talked together for hours at a time. This had been going on for years before we were married.

We broke up a few times and dated others, but whenever that happened, we missed each other terribly. Ultimately, we realized that life without each other would be a tragic mistake, and so to avoid disaster we married much sooner than we had originally planned. Joyce was only nineteen; I was twenty-one.

Over sixty years later, with two married children and seven grandchildren, we still cannot imagine what life would be without each other. And we still find each other irresistible.

But Joyce and I are not still in love because we were meant for each other. It might seem that way, but it isn't true. The reason we are in love is that we have consistently done things for each other that kept our love alive. For over sixty years we have been giving each other the Four Gifts of Love.

Before I tell you about these gifts and how they can guarantee your love for each other and the success of your marriage, let's look first at how the feeling of love works. What is it that made you fall in love with each other? What could cause you to lose that love?

Romantic Love and the Love Bank

The feeling of love—I call it *romantic love*—is quite predictable. It's that predictability that makes me so successful in saving marriages. I know what creates romantic love, what destroys it, and what can sustain it for a lifetime. And I use that knowledge to help married couples recapture romantic love for each other even after they think it's been lost for good.

I want you to acquire that same knowledge so that your marriage will be as fulfilling for you and your spouse as my marriage has been for Joyce and me. But in order to understand how romantic love works, you'll need to understand a concept I created back in the 1970s that I call the Love Bank.

There is a Love Bank inside each one of us. Our emotions use it to keep track of the way people treat us. Every person we've ever known has an account in our Love Bank, and their balances are determined by how we feel when we are with them. If someone makes us feel good, love units are deposited into their account. But if we feel bad around this person, love units are withdrawn. The better we feel, the more love units are deposited; the worse we feel, the more love units are withdrawn.

The Love Bank is the way our emotions keep track of how people treat us. Good experiences deposit "love units," leading us to like or even love a person. Bad experiences withdraw units, leading us to dislike or even hate a person.

Our emotions use the balance in each person's Love Bank account to advise us as to whether or not we should spend time with that person. And they do it by making us feel a certain way. When someone has a positive Love Bank balance—more deposits than withdrawals—our emotions encourage us to be with that person by making us "like" him or her. But when someone has a

In the mid-1970s, Dr. Harley created the Love Bank concept as a tool to help his clients understand how their actions affected their spouse's feelings for them. It also helped them understand their GOAL—to create a lifestyle of **EXCEPTIONAL CARE**, where the feeling of romantic love is sustained by making deposits and avoiding withdrawals.

negative balance—more withdrawals than deposits—our emotions encourage us to run for cover by causing us to "dislike" that person.

The larger the positive balance in someone's Love Bank account, the more attracted we feel to that person. For example, if 200 love units accumulate, we feel comfortable around that person; if 500 love units accumulate, we may consider that person to be one of our best friends.

But something special happens when the Love Bank balance of someone of the opposite sex reaches a critical threshold of, say, 1000 love units. Our emotions give us an extra incentive to spend as much time as possible with that person—even for the rest of our lives! And that's the feeling I call romantic love.

Of course, negative balances have the opposite effect. Just like a checking account, a Love Bank account can be in the red when love units continue to be withdrawn after none are left. If someone at work who's been annoying eventually has a Love Bank balance of negative 200, our emotions will make us feel uncomfortable whenever he's around, even when he's not doing anything annoying. And someone with a Love Bank balance of negative 500 will seem downright repulsive. Our emotions want us to avoid that person whenever possible.

When someone has a very large negative balance, say negative 1000 love units, our emotions go to great lengths to encourage us to avoid *all* contact. That's when we end up "hating" that person. It happens automatically if someone's balance in our Love Bank dips to that critical low point.

We don't end up reaching that hate threshold with most people because we stop having contact with them before their Love Bank balance falls that far. If you work with a very rude and inconsiderate person, you can request another office and simply avoid contact as much as possible. Even if it's your next-door neighbor, you can try to ignore that person or even move, if necessary.

In marriage, escape isn't so easy. And without escape, Love Bank withdrawals can be unrelenting.

If you're not filling each other's Love Banks as a couple, you're probably emptying them. When one of you neglects the other, resentment and conflict are not far behind, and hostility waits in the wings. Instead of correcting the mistake, you're tempted to argue about the problem. I hope you've never had a serious fight, but if you have, you know how quickly Love Bank deposits can turn into Love Bank withdrawals. As Love Bank balances turn negative, your emotional reactions encourage you to make matters worse. You don't feel like caring for each other; you feel like neglecting each other.

If you make withdrawals as a lifestyle in each other's Love Bank, eventually your emotions will scream, "Get out of there!" As you continue to make each other miserable, your Love Bank balance may eventually reach negative 1000, the hate threshold, and you'll feel incredibly repulsed by your spouse whenever he or she is around. That's when divorce or permanent separation starts to seem like the only reasonable way to escape the nightmare.

Permanent separation *isn't* the only way to escape from the negative Love Bank cycle. It's true that our emotions make it seem impossible to ever be in love again when Love Bank balances are negative, but I've seen it happen for thousands of couples. If we learn to care for each other despite our negative emotional reactions, deposits replace withdrawals. As negative balances turn positive, our emotional reactions change as well. We eventually stop feeling repulsed and we start feeling attracted instead. Then it's easy to do what it takes to sustain the feeling of romantic love.

If you are in love with each other today, you've learned to make Love Bank deposits and avoid withdrawals. But if you don't continue making deposits and avoiding withdrawals, you'll eventually dislike, or even hate, each other.

Many people, including some who consider themselves experts, don't think that romantic love *can* be sustained permanently in marriage. My personal experience is living proof that they're  wrong. My wife, Joyce, and I have been in love with each other throughout our entire marriage, and we're not alone. About 20 percent of all marriages are passionate throughout life. These are the couples who kept giving the gifts of care, protection, honesty, and time.

Romantic love *doesn't* have to fade away with time. You and your spouse can be as much in love 50 years from now as you are today—if you understand another kind of love.

Another Kind of Love: Caring Love

Romantic love is not the only meaning of love. There's another kind of love that is also very important in marriage. I call it caring love— a willingness to take time and make an effort to be a primary source of happiness and avoid being a source of unhappiness. While romantic love is a feeling, caring love is a decision.

People can have caring love in many kinds of relationships. The love you have for your children is caring love, and you may also care for your parents and close friends. In fact, you may care for people you don't even know when you decide to invest time and resources in charitable organizations that help those people. Caring love is expressed by your effort to improve the quality of life for others.

As committed as you might be to care for your spouse, you may not actually be building Love Bank balances with that effort. For example, a husband may show his care by purchasing jewelry for his wife. But what if his wife doesn't want jewelry? What if she craves some heart-to-heart conversation instead? If the husband is too busy to fill her need for conversation, his marriage will be headed for disaster, no matter how much jewelry he gives her.

Some marriage counselors think spouses simply need to know that they care for each other; that they want each other to be happy. But they're wrong. Knowing that you care isn't enough to sustain romantic love. I've counseled thousands of couples that care about each other but have still filed for divorce. Why? Because the way they try to care for each other failed a crucial test—it doesn't deposit enough love units to break through the romantic love threshold. The only way to achieve that crucial objective is to do more than just *try* to make your spouse happy: You must *succeed*.

Caring love creates romantic love when your care for each other is effective. And if you give each other the Four Gifts of Love, your romantic love for each other can be sustained throughout life.

Review: What Is the Definition of Romantic Love and Caring Love

This book defines romantic love as the *feeling* of being in love—finding someone irresistible. It's an incredible attraction for someone of the opposite gender that is unmistakable and can be measured.

In my counseling, I use a test created by Dr. Harley to determine if the plan we use is creating the feeling of love for the couple. If the plan is successful, the test score will indicate that the couple has fallen in love with each other. They will also report that they feel in love—some for the first time in their marriage!

The test is called the Love Bank Inventory. I won't list all of the items in the entire test, but here are some questions that get to the essence of what the feeling of romantic love really is:

- Do you usually have a good feeling whenever you think about your partner?
- Would you rather be with your partner than anyone else?

- Do you enjoy telling your partner your deepest feelings and most private experiences?
- Does your partner bring out the best in you?

The feeling of love is very fragile and, once it's destroyed, it's difficult to restore. But tens of thousands have proven that it cannot only be restored; it can be sustained for a lifetime if a couple is committed to another kind of love—caring love. Caring love is the decision to do what it takes to be a primary source of happiness and avoid being a source of unhappiness. It's what you'll be learning about in this book—it's putting all Four Gifts of Love into action.

> When a couple expresses their caring love, it helps create and sustain their romantic love.

The two kinds of love in marriage affect each other. When a couple expresses their caring love, it helps create and sustain their romantic love. And when they experience romantic love, it's much easier to express caring love. In other words, when couples make the decision to care for each other by giving the Four Gifts of Love, the feeling of romantic love is the effect or symptom. And when they're in love, giving these four gifts seems almost effortless.

Thought Questions

1. If you currently feel romantic love for your partner, can you now explain why you have that feeling? And if your partner is in love with you, do you understand why?

2. Can you identify one thing YOU did to your partner today that made a deposit into your account of his or her Love Bank? Can you identify one thing YOU did today that could have caused a withdrawal of love units? Don't worry if these are difficult questions because the concepts within the next chapters will help you become more aware of these love unit deposits and withdrawals.

4

Fulfilling Promises

Imagine this...on your wedding day, your spouse said, *I promise to care for you, protect you, be honest with you, and make our time together my highest priority*. But months after the ceremony you're still waiting for those promises to be fulfilled. Instead of caring, your spouse didn't try to meet your needs. Instead of protecting, your spouse made demands of you, showed disrespect, and became angry whenever things didn't go his or her way. Instead of being honest, your spouse lied to you. Instead of taking time to be with you, your spouse neglected you entirely. What good would those promises be to you if they were not fulfilled or even only partially fulfilled?

Marital promises to care, protect, give honesty, and time are an important first step toward making your marriage mutually fulfilling. They reflect your understanding of each other's expectations in marriage and your willingness to fulfill those expectations. But promises themselves only help set your goals in marriage. It's *doing* what was promised that makes you both happy.

So you need a plan of action that guarantees the implementation of your promises. A commitment to the Four Gifts of Love isn't about giving these gifts for a day, here or there—it's about continuously giving and receiving these gifts. It's about creating a lifestyle of gift-giving habits.

The Promise-Fulfilling Plan...Creating Habits

Almost everything we do is in the form of habits—*learned behaviors that are a repeated part of our lifestyle.* Think about how you brush your teeth, eat, or even fold your arms. How you do these tasks are examples of habits in your life. Many think that we use our intelligence and creativity to do what we do and say what we say. But the truth is that we automatically repeat ourselves far more often than we would like to admit.

Our behavior is repetitive because it takes less "gray matter," or brainpower, to function with habits. Quite frankly, if we didn't have habits to guide our behavior, our brains would have to be the size of buildings to make every one of our actions creative and intelligent. Since our brains are relatively small, our limited creativity and intelligence are reserved for new situations where no habits have yet formed, or when we want to change old habits into new habits.

Even though habits take less brainpower, they aren't mindless or meaningless. Habits take at least a moment of conscious choice to start. And they are started because they fulfill a purpose. Think again of the things you do *repeatedly* during your day: eat, drink, sleep, drive to work, brush your teeth, and dress. Each has a purpose and the way you do each habit started with a conscious decision.

Consider the habit of putting on socks. One purpose is to make shoes more comfortable. But there are many different ways to put on socks—before or after pants, rolled up or not rolled up before sliding them on, right or left foot first. For those who are in the habit of wearing socks, they chose a particular style at one point in time. After repeated practice, the chosen style eventually becomes a habit—something that feels natural.

Habits Affect Others

Can you see where I'm headed? Some of our habits, like putting on socks, don't seem relevant to your marriage. But habits are important in our discussions of what it takes to fulfill your promises to give care, protection, honesty, and time.

Specific and meaningful actions give the Four Gifts of Love. If those specific and meaningful actions become habits, then giving the Four Gifts of Love would become a regular part of your lifestyle— guaranteeing the fulfillment of your promises.

So what's the secret to creating a promise-fulfilling habit? It's very simple—if any particular behavior is repeated often enough, it becomes a habit. At first, the new behavior is usually awkward or even somewhat unpleasant each time you do it. But after you practice for a while, it becomes smooth and almost effortless—it becomes a habit.

Take brushing your teeth for example. You probably don't remember when you first learned how to brush your teeth, but maybe you've seen a toddler start the learning process. At first, a parent repeatedly shows how to put the toothpaste on the brush, hold the brush, place the brush in the mouth, and with a circular brushing action, move it along each tooth area. Eventually, the child does it independently and effortlessly—no longer is every aspect of the routine carefully thought through. It becomes a series of habits.

Keep in mind that forming a new habit is not always easy—it might even seem uncomfortable at first. That's simply because you are not used to it, but it should get easier and more comfortable once you practice the new behavior.

As we discuss the remaining concepts, keep in mind the value of a thoughtful habit and the harm of a thoughtless habit as you create a promise-fulfilling lifestyle.

Thought Questions

1. If you could create a new habit that would make your partner happy, would you do it?

2. If you had a habit that caused your partner to be unhappy, would you change it?

P.S. God is also committed to fulfilling His promises to those who are in a relationship with Him. The most important promise is that we will spend eternity with Him in Heaven. That promise will be fulfilled only after we die. But He has also made promises that can be fulfilled during our lifetime. He has promised to make our lives much more abundant and meaningful. And what's wonderful about God's promises is that He doesn't need to learn how to fulfill them—He's already an expert.

We, on the other hand, are not at all like God. Becoming a follower of Christ doesn't automatically and perfectly *make* us behave in ways that reflect His Lordship in our lives—obeying His commands to love Him with our heart, mind, and soul, and loving others because of our love for Him. We need a lot of help fulfilling our promises.

Fortunately, one of God's promises is that He will help us form a powerful life-changing partnership that transforms our lives. In fact, without Him, we could never come close to meeting His expectations.

God plays a major role in His partnership with us, but our action plan is still essential. In Psalm 127:1a we read, "Unless the Lord builds the house, the builders labor in vain." The Lord and we, "the builders," work together. It's our effort that becomes meaningful and productive when God is the general contractor. God provides guidance and the blueprint as we build a promise-fulfilling life.

PART ONE

The Gift of Care

I PROMISE TO BE A PRIMARY
SOURCE OF HAPPINESS BY MEETING
YOUR MOST IMPORTANT
EMOTIONAL NEEDS

5
What Is Care

What is care? That is a good question for a couple who promised or will promise to care for each other for a lifetime. But have you ever thought about what it means? And what does it look like in daily life?

Care is a word with many meanings in our language. When we say we care, it can mean that we are concerned about someone and hope that person will be happy in life. It can also mean that we have strong emotional feelings for a person. Or it's another way of saying that we're in love with someone.

However, I use the word care to mean what you do for each other, not how you hope or feel. Care, to me, is a willingness to take time and make an effort to be a source of happiness. When you promise to care for each other, you promise to do things that will enhance the quality and enjoyment of each other's life. It is part of the caring love I introduced to you previously.

You decided to marry because you probably found each other irresistible and you simply could not imagine living without each other. It's the Love Bank's fault. You managed to deposit so many love units into each other's Love Bank that you triggered the inevitable reaction of romantic love. And that feeling of love has encouraged you to spend the rest of your lives together.

It's the way you've cared for each other that helped create your feeling of romantic love. Your care deposited huge sums of love units in your Love Banks. But do you know what you did to deposit so many love units—and what you will need to do to continue depositing them? In this chapter, I will explain how your care for each other deposits the love units that create and maintain your love for each other. I will also show you how to keep them coming throughout your marriage.

As I've already said, romantic love is not a mystery; it's a predictable emotional reaction. The relationship between care and romantic love is also predictable. Care can help create romantic love. Lack of care can destroy it.

The Art of Caring

Some of us are naturally talented in making others feel good, but most of us have had to learn how to do it through trial and error. Fortunately, as children, we were usually quick to let each other know how we were being affected. When we did something others liked, we became their friends, and when we upset them, we became their enemies. But enemies could become friends and vice versa between recess and lunch. As children, we could redeem ourselves rather quickly if we had made a social blunder.

By the time we entered adolescence, most of us had established our social etiquette well enough to attract friends who remained friends for weeks, or even months, at a time. Some of these friends were of the opposite sex, and that added a new dimension to the meaning of friendship.

We discovered that at least some of our opposite-sex friends gave us feelings that we have never felt before—better than any we had ever experienced. We were used to friends making us feel good, but this was fantastic. Imagine, me, talking to a girl on the telephone for hours. I never did that with my best friend, Steve. Why did I do it with Joyce? Because it felt so good just to talk to her. And she apparently felt the same way. We were depositing love units into each other's Love Bank.

I could make Joyce very happy, but I could also upset her. I discovered that what wouldn't have bothered Steve much bothered Joyce quite a bit. And I seemed to be able to bother her almost effortlessly. My practical jokes were especially annoying to her. They often withdrew all the love units I had deposited when we talked on the telephone.

The most popular girls in my high school were those who knew how to make guys feel terrific. Quite frankly, their appearance usually had a lot to do with it, but they also had other traits that most boys found attractive. And the guys that were most popular among the girls were those who knew how to make girls feel great and sweep them off their feet. Those guys had learned the art of caring, the art of depositing love units. And they also knew how to avoid wrecking everything: They didn't torment their girlfriends with the practical jokes that I found so entertaining. Those of us who were not among the most popular would often try to copy what we thought the popular boys were doing. And most of us improved over time, eventually learning the art of caring love.

Care is definitely an art. You were artful enough to fall in love with each other. What did you do to deposit all those love units? What caused such a large deposit of love units to be made at one time that you broke through the romantic love threshold and fell in love? It took even me a while to answer that question during my first few years as a marriage counselor. But eventually, through the help of hundreds of people I counseled, I discovered what it was. If your marriage is to be as successful as you hoped it would be, you will need to discover it too. First, though, I should explain something that has a great deal to do with this art form—emotional needs.

What Is an Emotional Need

We all know about physical needs, such as the need for food, water, oxygen, warmth, and so forth. These are essential to our survival. With them, our bodies thrive. Without them, we die.

There is also another kind of need that all of us have—emotional needs. When these needs are not met, we don't die, but some of us may wish we could. An emotional need is a craving that, when satisfied, leaves us feeling happy and content. When it's unsatisfied, we feel unhappy and frustrated.

> Emotional Need: a **craving** that, when satisfied, leaves us feeling happy and content. When it's unsatisfied, we feel unhappy and frustrated.

Most physical needs are also emotional needs. Physical deprivation leads to emotional craving, and physical satisfaction leads to emotional contentment. Food is a good example. When we're hungry, a physical need for food is accompanied by an emotional craving for food. The same thing is true of water.

But not every physical need is also an emotional need. For example, we need oxygen, but we don't have an emotional reaction every time the need is not met. We can breathe, say, helium instead of oxygen and feel okay right up until we pass out. Oxygen is a physical need without an emotional component.

On the other hand, many emotional needs are not physical needs. What makes us feel good in life often has nothing to do with our physical well-being. In fact, there are many emotional needs that, when met, actually threaten our physical health. For example, we put our health at risk when we satisfy an emotional craving for drugs and alcohol.

There are probably thousands of emotional needs—a need for birthday parties (or at least birthday presents), peanut butter sandwiches, watching sports, and so forth. Whenever one of our emotional needs is met, we feel good, and when it's not met, we feel bad. Try telling a sports fan that he (or she) can't watch any sports this week, and you get a taste of how emotional needs affect people.

Not all emotional needs affect us with the same intensity. Some make us feel very good when met and very bad when unmet. Others have a very small effect on us. In other words, meeting some needs deposit many love units, while meeting others deposit only a  few. But there are a few emotional needs that, when met, deposit so many love units that we fall in love with the person who meets them. These are the ones you met for each other during courtship, and you did such a good job meeting them that you fell in love. I call these needs the *most important emotional needs.*

Care Means Meeting the Most Important Emotional Needs

When you come right down to it, your promise to care for each other is a promise to meet each other's most important emotional needs. This is what you expect of each other after you're married. But right now, you may not know what they are. And even if you do know what they are today, they're likely to change in the future, especially after you have children.

So let me introduce to you the ten emotional needs that are usually very important in marriage. They are affection, sexual fulfillment, intimate conversation, recreational companionship, honesty and openness, physical attractiveness, financial support, domestic support, family commitment, and admiration. When these needs are met in a marriage, spouses can experience great pleasure, and when they are not met, spouses experience frustration and disappointment.

Whereas almost everyone has these ten needs to some extent, people vary greatly in the way they are affected by them. For some, when the need for affection is met, a great deal of pleasure is felt, while for others, affection doesn't do much for them. The same can be said for admiration: Some need it greatly, while others don't.

While this list identifies the most common important emotional needs, all ten are not usually important to any one person. In fact,  I've found that, in general, only five out of the ten are identified by a person as important enough to create the feeling of romantic love when they are met. In other words, only five have the potential for depositing enough love units to break through the romantic love threshold. That being the case, it makes sense to put maximum effort into meeting each other's top five emotional needs.

It's not that difficult to preserve the feeling of romantic love you have for each other if you focus your attention on each other's five most important emotional needs. But which of these needs are most important to your partner? Which five are most important to you? It's very likely that the ones you pick will not be the same as the ones your partner picks. One of the most important discoveries I made early in my counseling career was that men and women tend to prioritize these ten needs very differently.

Men *tend* to give the highest priority to:

1. sexual fulfillment
2. recreational companionship
3. physical attractiveness
4. domestic support
5. admiration

These are the emotional needs that, when met, cause most men to fall in love with the woman who meets them. Women, on the other hand, *tend* to give the highest priority to:

1. affection
2. intimate conversation
3. honesty and openness
4. financial support
5. family commitment

These are the emotional needs that, when met, cause most women to fall in love with the man who meets them. Of course, not every man or woman prioritizes their needs exactly the same way. Some men consider affection or intimate conversation to be one of their top five needs, and some women rank admiration and sexual fulfillment among their most important needs. But on average, I've found that men and women rank these needs the way I listed them.

Since men and women tend to prioritize their emotional needs so differently, it's no wonder they have difficulty adjusting to each other in marriage. If a man assumes that his wife's most important emotional needs are similar to his, he will fail miserably when he tries to meet them. A woman will fail if she makes the same assumption.

> Not every man or woman prioritizes their needs exactly the same way.

I have seen this simple error threaten many marriages. A husband and wife fail to meet each other's emotional needs not because they're selfish or uncaring, but because they are ignorant of what those needs are.

He may think he is doing her a big favor by inviting her to play golf with him (recreational companionship, one of his top needs), but she'll come home thoroughly frustrated because he didn't talk with her enough while they played (intimate conversation, one of her top needs). She hopes to please him by showering him with affection (which meets her need) but ends up frustrating him because her affection arouses his sexual interest (his need for sex), and that's not what she had in mind. Both spouses think they are valiantly trying to meet the other's needs, but they are aiming at the wrong target.

Question: Where should you put your greatest effort so that you can deposit the most love units?

Answer: Meet each other's most important emotional needs.

Question: How can you discover which needs are the most important to each of you?

Answer: Ask.

As I've explained, you cannot assume that your partner's emotional needs have the same priority as yours. You are the only one who can identify your most important emotional needs, and your partner is the expert on his or her needs. You must ask if you want to know where to put your greatest effort. Before you ask, though, I'd like you to become familiar with the choices, so in the next chapter, we'll take a closer look at the ten emotional needs I listed. Then I'll explain how to decide which needs are the most important to meet, will deposit the most love units, and will demonstrate your care for each other.

Giving the gift of care starts with a *decision* and *willingness* to be a primary source of happiness for your spouse and then it's your *effort* that puts your willingness into action.

Giving the gift of care starts with a *decision* and *willingness* to be a primary source of happiness for your spouse and then it's your *effort* that puts your willingness into

⚙ *Talk About This*

Reminder: Please keep the conversation **BRIEF** and **STAY ON** the topic of the questions. And most importantly, use this time to practice your gifts of care and protection, being especially careful to avoid disrespectful comments. Remember, your goals are to be a source of happiness and avoid being a source of pain in your marriage.

1. Would you be disappointed if, after you were married, your spouse stated that he or she would not meet some of your most important emotional needs?

2. What is one of the best experiences you have had with your partner? What did he or she do to make you feel so good?

3. Can you recite the definition of an emotional need without looking? (Hint: craving, satisfied, happy, unsatisfied, unhappy)

6

Most Important Emotional Needs, Part I

As Mary confided in some friends about her lack of feelings for Dennis, it became clear that the loss of love seemed to be considered a normal process of maturing in marriage. One friend even jokingly said, "Congratulations! You are now officially married." Another friend had Mary questioning if her marriage was "right" for her. "What?" Mary thought. These were *not* the answers she wanted to hear, and thankfully she didn't accept them.

Instead, Mary confided in Dennis, and they got advice from another friend that encouraged them to learn about the Love Bank and emotional needs. It was as if a light bulb went on for both of them. They were now able to explain what was causing their loss of love. This was also a huge relief. Their change in feelings for each other was not a sign that they shouldn't be together or that their marriage was now "maturing." It was a symptom of their neglect in meeting each other's most important emotional needs.

But before Dennis and Mary could meet those needs, they first had to learn about themselves and ask, "What are my most important emotional needs in marriage?" They had never considered that question before now.

Do you know yourself well enough to list your most important emotional needs? Most people haven't given this much thought and, if forced to make up a list, would not know where to begin. But it's very important to understand your emotional needs, not only for your own sake but for the sake of your spouse. If he or she is to put time and energy into becoming an expert at meeting those needs, you'd better be sure you've identified the right ones. And it's also important for you to understand your partner's emotional needs so that you too can put your effort in the right places.

Introducing the Very Important Emotional Needs

To help you identify your most important emotional needs, you can choose from the list of ten I have already presented. But my list of needs may not include all of the needs that are most important to you.

Ambition is a good example of a need that I have excluded from my list of ten needs. Some people gain tremendous pleasure from the ambition of their spouse. As long as their spouse continues to achieve important objectives, love units keep pouring in. But I found that need to be so uncommon that it did not make my final cut. In your case, however, if it makes your cut, you may want to include it along with a few others in your list of most important emotional needs. But only do so if it seems to have caused you to fall in love with someone who met that need.

For most of us, the ten needs we're about to discuss will cover the bases. I'll describe each of them for you so you can determine which five are most important to you. Remember, *craving* is an important aspect of a need. If you have a craving for any of the following, it should be on your list. And *frustration* is another important aspect. If you are frustrated when one of the following needs is not met, it's likely to be one of your most important emotional needs.

Affection

The need for affection is a craving to receive nonsexual expressions of care symbolizing security, protection, and comfort, which may include words, cards, gifts, hugs, kisses, and courtesies.

Affection communicates the following messages: "I'll care for you and protect you"; "You're valuable to me"; "I'm concerned about the problems you face"; "I will help you overcome those problems;" and "I'm thinking about you." A simple hug can say those things. When we hug our friends and relatives, we are expressing our care for them. And there are other ways to show our affection: a greeting card, a thoughtful gift, an "I love you" note, a bouquet of flowers, holding hands, back rubs, a phone message or text saying, "I'm thinking about you," and a loving tone can all communicate affection.

Affection is, for many, the essential cement of a relationship. Without it, many people feel totally alienated. With it, they become emotionally bonded to the one showing the affection. If you feel terrific when you receive affection and feel frustrated when you don't, you have the emotional need for affection and it should be on your list.

Anyone can learn to be affectionate. It's a matter of learning new habits that will make you an affectionate spouse. Here are some habits one wife *suggested* to her husband: hug and kiss me every morning while we're still in bed; tell me that you love me while we're having breakfast; call me during the day to see how I'm doing; bring me flowers once a month as a surprise; help me with the dishes; put our arm around me and hold my hand when we're sitting together; and hug and kiss me every night before going to sleep.

Thought Questions

1. If your partner stopped giving you acts of affection, would that bother you? Yes or No?

2. If your answer is "yes" to the above question, this is probably one of your most important emotional needs. If this is one of your most important emotional needs, begin thinking of specific ways you enjoy having this need met.

Sexual Fulfillment

The need for sexual fulfillment is a craving to engage in an enjoyable sexual experience.

Sex and affection are often confused, especially by men. This distinction should help you: Affection is an act of love that is nonsexual and can be given to and received from friends, relatives, children, and even pets with absolutely no sexual connotation. However, if the act of love is done with a sexual motive, or has sexual overtones, it's sex, not affection.

A sexual need usually predates your relationship with each other and is somewhat independent of your relationship. If you have experienced a craving for sex before you met, you probably have a sexual need. While you may have discovered a deep desire to make love to your partner when you are in love, it may not reflect an underlying emotional need for sexual fulfillment.

Sexual fantasies are usually a good indicator of a sexual need. If you tend to imagine having a sexual experience when you daydream, sexual fulfillment is probably one of your important emotional needs. Incidentally, in general, dominant fantasies usually reflect emotional needs.

When you marry, you promise to be faithful to each other for life. This means that you will be each other's only sexual partner "until death do you part." You will make this commitment because you trust each other to meet your sexual needs, being sexually available and responsive.

The need for sexual fulfillment is a very exclusive need. If you have it, you will be very dependent on your spouse to meet it for you. If your spouse has this need, he/she will be dependent on you to meet it.

But that commitment for sexual exclusivity should go beyond being faithful. It also means avoiding any sexual activities and experiences that might compete and interfere with the sexual experiences you have with each other. On a psychological note, it creates a contrast effect where those experiences will be compared to the experiences with your spouse. Involvement with pornography, strip clubs, masturbation, and other forms of non-marital sexual gratification should be avoided at all costs because they will dilute Love Bank deposits when you make love to each other. If you want your marriage to be passionate throughout your lives, don't let anything compete with the experience you have with each other.

The three aspects of sexual fulfillment include: 1) quality—a predictably enjoyable experience; 2) quantity—a frequency that satisfies you (not a special event, but a *regularly* planned event); and 3) mutuality—you both respond sexually and find the frequency satisfying.

How can a couple achieve sexual compatibility? Remember this is a process of learning for a husband and wife. The first step is to overcome your sexual ignorance. A husband and wife must learn to understand their own sexual responses and what triggers them. Second, you need to communicate your sexual understanding to each other. A husband and wife should share what they know about their own sexual response. Finally, you should both create conditions that guarantee a mutually enjoyable sexual response that is as often as either of you would like it to be.

It is also important to understand that there are five stages in a sexual experience:

1. Desire or Willingness: Wanting or being willing to engage in sex, but not yet being sexually aroused. Most men are likely to experience desire, which is triggered by the hormone testosterone. For most women, this stage takes the form of willingness more than desire, which is triggered by affection, attentiveness, kindness, and a previously enjoyable sexual experience.

2. Arousal: The beginning of sexual feelings (associated with a partial erection for men and lubrication of the vagina for women). Most men are aroused by each of many senses. For most women, tactile stimulation is most important (where the husband touches his wife).

3. Plateau: Intense sexual feelings (associated with an involuntary full erection and tightening of the vagina).

4. Climax: Most intense sexual feeling (associated with ejaculation for men and pulsing vagina for women). Most men are capable of only one. Most women are capable of many.

5. Recovery: Relaxing following climax. Men often lose sexual motivation suddenly and almost completely. Most women retain their sexual feelings and remain aroused for about 20 minutes after climax.

Remember that the sexual experience is different for men and women. Spouses should teach each other about their own sexual reactions in an attempt to create a mutually enjoyable experience for each of the five stages.

Sex should never be unpleasant or forced. Unpleasant experiences make a spouse less willing to continue meeting the need. On the other hand, if each spouse is thoughtful of the other, creating a mutually pleasant experience of care, this need will be met willingly throughout your marriage.

Thought Questions

1. If your partner indicated that he/she didn't plan on having a sexual relationship with you when married, would that have affected your decision to marry? Yes or No?

2. Do you expect your spouse to engage in a sexual relationship with you throughout your marriage? Yes or No?

3. If you are married and your answers are "yes" to the above questions, this is probably one of your most important emotional needs.

4. If you are engaged and your answers are "yes" to the above questions, this is not a current most important emotional need, but when married it will most likely become one of your most important emotional needs

Intimate Conversation

The need for intimate conversation is a craving to share feelings, personal experiences, topics of personal interest, opinions, and plans with another.

Unlike sex, conversation is not a need that's usually met exclusively in marriage. Our need for conversation can be ethically met by almost anyone. But *intimate* conversation, in which you talk about very personal problems and feelings, can meet such an important emotional need that you're likely to fall in love with a person of the opposite sex who meets it. If you crave intimate conversation, be sure that your partner is the only one of the opposite sex who meets that need.

Men and women don't have too much difficulty talking to each other during courtship. That's a time of information gathering for both partners. Both are highly motivated to discover each other's likes and dislikes, personal background, current interests and problems, and plans for the future.

But after marriage, many women find that the man who, before marriage, would spend hours talking to her now seems to have lost all interest in talking and spends his spare time watching television or reading. Don't let that common problem in marriage happen to you. Make sure that the great conversations you have shared during your courtship will continue throughout your marriage.

The reality is that it takes time to talk. So don't try to meet this need on the run. Deep and intimate conversation between a husband and wife requires privacy and planning. Otherwise, you will not be able to solve problems, plan, negotiate, understand each other, and create an emotional bond.

The friends of good conversation are:

- Using conversation to get-to-know the other person more deeply, inform, and understand each other
- Developing interest in each other's favorite topics of conversation
- Balancing conversation
- Giving each other undivided attention

The enemies of good conversation are:

- Using conversation to try to get your way at your partner's expense (selfish demands)

- Using conversation to force agreement to your way of thinking (disrespectful judgments)

- Using conversation to punish your partner (angry outbursts)

- Dwelling on mistakes, past or present

If you see conversation as a practical necessity, primarily as a means to an end, you probably don't have much of a need for it. But if you pick up the telephone just because you feel like talking – to anyone – about the events of your day, your personal feelings and problems, topics of interest, and plans for the future consider it to be one of your most important emotional needs.

Thought Questions

1. About how many hours per week do you spend in conversation with your partner? Is this enough? Would you like the quality of your conversation to be different?

2. If this is one of your most important emotional needs, begin thinking of specific ways you enjoy having this need met. One way to increase the quality of your conversation is to download and use the E^2: Explore and Engage mobile app from FourGiftsofLove.org, Google Play, and Apple App Store.

Recreational Companionship

The need for recreational companionship is a craving to engage in recreational activities with at least one other person.

A need for recreational companionship combines two needs into one. First, there is the need to be engaged in recreational activities, and second, the need to have a companion. To determine if you have this need, first ask yourself if you have a craving for certain recreational activities. Then ask yourself if the activities require a companion for fulfillment. If the answer is "yes" to both questions, recreational companionship should be on your list.

During your courtship, you and your partner probably had been each other's favorite recreational companion. It's not uncommon for a woman to join a man in hunting, fishing, watching football, or other activities she would never have chosen on her own. She simply wants to spend as much time as possible with the man she likes, and that means going where he likes to go.

The same is true of a man. Shopping centers are no strangers to a man in love. He will also take his date out to dinner, watch romantic movies, and attend concerts and plays. A man and woman in love take whatever opportunity there is to be together and to be certain that their partner wants more dates in the future.

I won't deny that marriage changes a relationship considerably. But does it have to bring an end to the activities that helped make the relationship so compatible? Can't a husband's favorite recreational companion be his wife and vice versa? Think about it for a moment in terms of the Love Bank. How much do you enjoy these activities and how many love units would your partner be depositing if you enjoyed them together? What a waste it would be if someone else got credit for all those love units. And if it were someone of the opposite sex, it would be downright  dangerous. Who should get credit for all those love units? The one you should love the most: Your spouse. That's precisely why I encourage couples to be each other's favorite recreational companion. It's one of the simplest ways to make Love Bank deposits.

There are thousands of recreational activities that you would enjoy if you tried them, and thousands that your partner would enjoy. And of those thousands, there are hundreds of recreational activities you would enjoy together. Since you have time for just a few of these mutually enjoyable activities, why waste your time on those that only one of you enjoys?

How do you find mutually enjoyable recreational interests? An important policy that I teach couples to follow is called the Policy of Mutual Appeal—*engage in only those recreational activities that both you and your spouse can enjoy together.* The first step is to discover those mutually enjoyable recreational interests.

If you are to become each other's favorite recreational companions, spend almost all of your leisure time with each other to develop those mutual recreational interests.

Thought Questions

1. If you crave recreational activities and someone must join you for them to be fulfilling, this is one of your most important emotional needs.

2. If this is one of your most important emotional needs, try to identify five activities that you mutually enjoy.

The Four Intimate Emotional Needs

Before I describe the six remaining emotional needs, give special attention to the four that have just been reviewed. I've found these four to be so important in marriage that, unless all of them are met, marriage is rarely satisfying to both spouses. That's because they usually make the largest Love Bank deposits when met.

Men usually identify sexual fulfillment and recreational companionship as their two most important emotional needs, and women usually choose affection and conversation as their most important. When all four are met in marriage, both husband and wife usually find themselves emotionally fulfilled and in love.

I also recommend reading my book, *His Needs, Her Needs: Making Romantic Love Last* (Harley, 1986, 2022) for more information on all the emotional needs in marriage.

7

Most Important Emotional Needs, Part II

There was a time when I was so impressed with the results of spouses who met only the four intimate emotional needs that I wondered why I should encourage them to try to meet any of the rest. But over the years I've found the remaining six to be valuable enough in marriage that I include them for both romantic and practical reasons. As you read their descriptions, choose the ones that are the most important to you, and add them to your list, keeping in mind that the first four are absolutely essential for a healthy marriage. Whatever other needs you may have, you cannot afford to neglect meeting those four needs for each other throughout your lives together.

Honesty and Openness

The need for honesty and openness is a craving for truthful and frank expression of positive and negative feelings, events of the past, daily events and schedules, and plans for the future; not leaving a false impression.

Most people want an honest relationship with their partner. But some people have an emotional need for such a relationship. Honesty and openness help give them a sense of security—and make massive Love Bank deposits.

To feel secure, we want accurate information about our partner's thoughts, feelings, habits, likes, dislikes, personal history, daily activities, and plans for the future. If a partner does not provide honest and open communication, trust can be undermined and the feeling of security can eventually be destroyed. Then we can't trust the signals that are being sent and we have no foundation on which to build a solid relationship. Instead of adjusting, we feel off-balance; instead of growing together, we grow apart and incompatibility is created. In my experience, there is no room for privacy in marriage.

Aside from the practical advantages of honesty and openness, you may find that you feel happy and fulfilled when you and your partner reveal your most private thoughts to each other. You may also feel very frustrated when these thoughts are hidden. That reaction is evidence of an emotional need, one that can and should be met in marriage.

Thought Question

1. When your partner shares his/her most private thoughts and plans with you, does that make you happy? If so, this may be one of your most important emotional needs.

Physical Attractiveness

The need for physical attractiveness is a craving to observe someone whose appearance is aesthetically and/or sexually pleasing to you.

For many, physical attractiveness can be one of the greatest sources of Love Bank deposits. If you have this need, an attractive person will not only get your attention but may distract you from whatever it was you were doing. In fact, that's what may have first drawn you to your spouse: his or her physical attractiveness.

There are some who consider this need to be temporary and important only at the beginning of a relationship. After a couple gets to know each other better, some feel that physical attractiveness should take a back seat to deeper and more intimate needs.

But that's not been my experience, nor has it been the experience of many whom I've counseled, particularly men. For many individuals, the need for an attractive spouse continues throughout marriage, and love units continue to be deposited whenever the spouse is seen.

Ninety percent of the complaints I've heard regarding physical attractiveness are about excess weight. If spouses would simply maintain a healthy diet and exercise, making sure that they don't gain weight from year to year, most of them would remain physically attractive to each other throughout their lives.

Personal hygiene, physical fitness, weight, tone of voice, and choice of clothing, hairstyle, fragrance, and makeup (for a woman) all affect a person's attractiveness. It can be very subjective, and you are the judge of what is attractive to you.

Thought Questions

1. If the attractiveness of your partner makes you feel great, and the loss of that attractiveness would make you feel very frustrated, then this may be one of your most important emotional needs.

2. Think about the aspects of your partner's physical appearance that are important. What makes him/her physically attractive to you?

Financial Support

The need for financial support is a craving to receive help with financial resources to house, feed, and clothe your family.

Is financial support one of your important emotional needs? What if, before your marriage, your partner tells you not to expect any income from him or her? Would it affect your decision to marry? Or what if after marriage your spouse cannot find work, and you must financially support him or her throughout life? Would that cause frustration?

What constitutes financial support? Earning enough to buy everything you could possibly desire or earning just enough to get by? People answer this question differently, and the same person might have one answer in one stage of life, and other answers at other stages. Think about what your needs are now and what they may be in the future. What would you expect in order to feel fulfilled? What would disappoint you?

Like many of these emotional needs, financial support is sometimes difficult to discuss. As a result, many couples begin marriage with hidden expectations and assumptions. These can turn into resentment if they go unfulfilled.

You may have a need for financial support if you expect your spouse to earn a living, and you definitely have that need if you do not expect to be earning a living yourself, at least while raising your children. Express this need clearly and you're more likely to have it fulfilled.

Thought Questions

1. If your partner indicated that he/she didn't plan on earning an income, would that have affected your decision to marry? Yes or No?

2. Do you expect your spouse to earn a living throughout your marriage until retirement and don't expect yourself to earn a living, at least for part of your marriage? Yes or No?

3. If you are married and your answers are "yes" to the above questions, this is probably one of your most important emotional needs.

4. If you are engaged and your answers are "yes" to the above questions, this will not be a current most important emotional need, but when married it will most likely become one of your most important emotional needs.

Domestic Support

The need for domestic support is a craving to receive help with household tasks and care of the children (if any are at home).

The need for domestic support is a time bomb. At first, it seems irrelevant, a throwback to more primitive times. But for many couples, the need explodes after a few years of marriage, surprising both spouses.

In earlier generations, it was assumed that all husbands had this need and all wives would cheerfully meet it. Times have changed, and emotional needs have changed along with them. Now many of the men I counsel would rather have their wives meet their needs for affection or intimate conversation, needs that have traditionally been more characteristic of women. And many women, especially those with full-time careers, gain a great deal of pleasure from having their husbands help around the house and look after the children.

Marriage usually begins with a willingness of both spouses to share domestic responsibilities. Newlyweds commonly wash dishes together, make the bed together, and divide many household tasks. The groom welcomes the help he gets from his wife with the chores he's been doing alone as a bachelor. At this point in marriage, neither of them would identify domestic support as an important emotional need. But the time bomb is ticking.

When does the need for domestic support explode? When children arrive! Children create huge needs: A greater need for income and more demanding domestic responsibilities. The previous division of labor becomes obsolete. Both spouses must take on new responsibilities. Which ones will they take?

Right now, you may think you have no need for domestic support at all. But that may change later, and when it does, be ready to make up a new list of emotional needs. In fact, as soon as you expect to have your first child, you will find yourselves changing your priorities dramatically. What household tasks are you unwilling to assume? How much childcare do you expect your spouse to provide? And if your spouse were to assume some of those responsibilities, how much pleasure would you experience?

Meeting the need for domestic support involves help with creating a peaceful and well-managed home environment. But meeting this need doesn't mean that you do all the work. It simply means that you are doing domestic activities that mean the most to him or her (making love unit deposits).

> Meeting the need for domestic support involves help with creating a peaceful and well-managed home environment. But meeting this need doesn't mean that you do all the work. It simply means that you are doing domestic activities that mean the most to him or her (making love unit deposits).

Thought Questions

1. If your partner indicated that he/she didn't plan to provide any domestic support, would that have affected your decision to marry? Yes or No?

2. Do you expect your spouse to be primarily responsible for domestic activities throughout your marriage? Yes or No?

3. If you are married and your answers are "yes" to the above questions, this is probably one of your most important emotional needs.

4. If you are engaged and your answers are "yes" to the above questions, this will not be a current most important emotional need, but when married it will most likely become one of your most important emotional needs, especially when children arrive.

Family Commitment

The need for family commitment is a craving to receive help with the moral and educational development of your children within the family unit.

In addition to a greater need for income and help with domestic responsibilities, the arrival of children creates in many people the need for family commitment. Evidence of this need is a craving for your spouse's involvement in the educational and moral development of your children. When he or she helps care for them, you will feel very fulfilled, and when he or she doesn't, you will feel very frustrated.

Family commitment is not childcare. Feeding, clothing, or watching over children to keep them safe is childcare and falls under the category of domestic support. Family commitment, on the other hand, is taking responsibility for the development of the children and teaching them values that will help them become successful adults. It may include reading to them, taking them on frequent outings, developing the skills in appropriate child-training methods, and discussing those methods with you.

As with domestic support, you may not have this need if you do not have a child. But when your first child is born, a change may take place that you didn't anticipate. When you begin to crave your spouse's participation in the training of your child, it becomes an emotional need for you. Be sure to communicate that fact to your spouse and add it to the list of your most important emotional needs.

Thought Questions

1. If your partner indicated that he/she didn't plan on being actively involved in raising your children, would that have affected your decision to marry? Yes or No?

2. Do you expect your spouse to be actively involved in the development and education of your children? Yes or No?

3. If you have children and your answers are "yes" to the above questions, this is probably one of your most important emotional needs.

4. If you do not have children and your answers are "yes" to the above questions, this will not be a current most important emotional need, but when you have children, it will most likely become one of your most important emotional needs.

Admiration

The need for admiration is a craving to be shown respect, value, and appreciation.

If you have the need for admiration, one of the reasons you fell in love with your spouse may be that he or she compliments you. He or she may also be careful not to criticize you because criticism hurts you deeply.

Many of us have a need to be respected, valued, and appreciated, especially by the one we love. We want to be affirmed clearly and often. There's nothing wrong with feeling that way.

The need for admiration is one of the easiest emotional needs to meet. Just a compliment or word of praise, and "presto," you've made someone's day. On the other hand, it's also just as easy to be critical. A trivial word of rebuke can be very upsetting to people with this need, ruining their day and withdrawing love units at an alarming rate.

Thought Questions

1. When your partner gives you a compliment, does that make you happy? When he or she fails to compliment you or criticizes you are you frustrated?

2. If words of praise and criticism easily affect you, admiration may be one of your most important emotional needs.

Becoming an Expert

The ten emotional needs that I've just described are important to all of us. But only a few of the ten are so important to you that you will fall in love with the person that meets them.

Most of our happiness in life comes from our relationships with others. That's because we can't meet our most important emotional needs by ourselves; others must meet them for us. And we usually fall in love with and marry the person we think will do the very best job meeting them. Becoming each other's greatest source of happiness is a goal before marriage and should continue throughout life.

Why don't more spouses try to become experts at meeting each other's emotional needs? Being an expert simply means that you have made an effort to learn what to do (i.e., developed habits) to make each other happy and you do it very well. It's not really that difficult. In fact, the secrets of a happy marriage are fairly easy to discover, if people would simply educate themselves. Marriage requires basic skills for success. People take courses regularly to become experts at all sorts of things: computer programming, business management, and hairstyling. The wise couple will learn how to meet each other's emotional needs at an expert level and keep their skills finely tuned throughout their lives, sustaining a marriage that is as fulfilling as possible for both spouses.

But a word of caution: If a need is so important to you that you're likely to fall in love with the one who meets it, that need should be met exclusively in marriage. Why? Because if someone of the opposite sex meets that need, you are at risk of having an affair— one of the worst ways to betray your spouse. When you marry, you should give each other an exclusive right to meet your most important intimate emotional needs so you will love each other exclusively.

This exclusive right to meet each other's important intimate emotional needs places responsibility on your shoulders to meet those needs. After all, if your spouse promises not to let anyone else meet those needs, and then you fail to meet them yourself, your spouse will be in a very unpleasant and frustrating situation.

> When you marry, you should give each other an exclusive right to meet your most important intimate emotional needs so you will love each other exclusively.

Sexual fulfillment is one of the more obvious intimate emotional needs that should be met exclusively in marriage, but there are others that can be just as significant. For example, an affair doesn't usually begin with sex; it begins with the most intimate form of conversation, where personal feelings and problems are shared. If conversation can cause you to fall in love with someone of the opposite sex, your most intimate conversation should be limited to your spouse. The same is true of affection and recreational companionship. If you let someone other than your spouse meet those needs, you'll risk having an affair – one of the worst mistakes you could ever make in life.

Thought Questions

1. What do you think about the idea of a couple giving each other the exclusive right to meet their most important emotional needs, so that they will love each other exclusively? What would happen if someone of the opposite sex were to meet those needs? How would it affect the Love Bank account for that person? What would be a potential consequence?

2. What responsibility does the exclusive right to meet emotional needs imply? What is the responsibility of the one with the emotional needs? What is the responsibility of the one meeting the emotional needs?

8

Identifying Your Most
Important Emotional Needs

W hat are your most important emotional needs? Only you can identify them. And your partner is the only one who can identify his or her needs. Though I may know the average person's needs of highest priority, I don't know them for a certain individual until that person tells me what they are.

It's difficult for most people to identify their emotional needs without a little help. In the previous chapters, I introduced you to some of the most common emotional needs. From that list of ten needs, you were encouraged to select those that you know are important to you. If you haven't done so already, write down the needs you think are most important.

Remember, an emotional need is a **craving** that, when met, makes you feel happy and fulfilled, and when unmet makes you feel unhappy and frustrated. Try to determine what gives you the most pleasure when you have it, and what creates the most frustration when you don't have it. Those are your most important emotional needs.

You may add to your list emotional needs that are more important to you than those I included in the previous chapters. Try to think of things your partner could do for you that you crave most in life. If those needs are not included among the ten I've listed, and you are likely to fall in love with someone who meets those needs, they should be on your list. And they should be defined as clearly as possible so that your partner will understand what they are and know how to meet them. But don't include needs that you can meet on your own; select those needs that can be met only by someone else.

To help prepare you for this ranking process, imagine for a moment that your partner is willing to meet **only one** of the needs on your list and is unwilling to meet any of the rest. If that were the case, which one of the emotional needs would you select?

Before you answer, consider this: For the married spouse, if you don't choose sexual fulfillment as the most important need, you and your spouse may never have sex together. If you don't choose affection, your spouse may never hug or kiss you. If you don't choose financial support, your spouse may not earn a dime throughout your life together. If your spouse meets only one of the needs and all the other nine are left unmet, which would give you the most satisfaction and the least frustration? Which would deposit the most love units? The need you select should be ranked number 1.

As you know, your marriage will not survive if only one of your needs is met. So if you were able to choose one more need from the list, remembering that all the others would be unmet by your spouse, which would you choose? That need should be ranked number 2. Continue ranking your needs in order of their importance to you until you have chosen five. Each time you choose one, remember to consider all the others to be lost causes.

After you have ranked your top five emotional needs, I encourage you to take one last look and give special attention to those you didn't include. If all five of the needs you've listed are met by your spouse, will you be happy? If your spouse fails to meet a need that is not included on your list, will it threaten to ruin your marriage? If there is a sixth need that you feel must be included to ensure the success of your marriage, add it to the list. But then let your partner also add a sixth need to his or her list.

For the sake of the engaged couple using this material, your current need ranking will most likely change after marriage: Financial Support, Sexual Fulfillment, Domestic Support, and Family Commitment may not be on the current list, but will probably be added to either spouse's top five most important emotional needs after marriage.

For married couples, the ranking and/or the most important emotional needs can also change in life. This is why I will encourage every couple to revisit the list every year.

I've found that if a couple does an outstanding job meeting each other's top two emotional needs, they usually deposit enough love units to ensure romantic love. If couples do a reasonably good job meeting the other three, they add insurance to their marriage. But couples who try to meet all ten needs try to do too much and usually end up doing a poor or mediocre job on all of them. In those marriages, even though a great deal of effort is made, the results are very disappointing. So by focusing attention on the needs that mean the most, and ignoring the rest, couples can have sensational marriages.

Give very special attention to the needs you and your partner rank number 1 and number 2. Those are the needs you want to be experts in meeting for each other. If you leave them unmet in your marriage, your love for each other will be at risk. If someone outside the marriage meets them, he or she will become so attractive as to threaten your marriage. Affairs are particularly tempting when someone outside the marriage meets one of the two most important emotional needs that are unmet in marriage.

Agree to Meet Each Other's Needs

When you and your partner have identified your five (or six) emotional needs, I suggest that you commit to caring for each other by meeting the most important emotional needs. To help clarify this commitment, I've included a Marital Promise at the end of this book. You may list your needs as a reminder of your gift of care to each other.

It would be wise to review your list every year, because needs change over time, especially if you are engaged. Some years the change may not be very great, maybe just a reordering of needs. But for example, in the year a couple has their first child, new needs may completely replace some of the old ones. In these situations, couples must remind themselves that *care* means meeting each other's most important emotional needs, even when those needs change during your lifetime together. And to know what they are, you will need to check with each other regularly.

Evaluate Your Effectiveness

Most people feel that they can meet their spouse's emotional needs if they simply know what they are. Affection, intimate conversation, recreational companionship – these shouldn't be too difficult to manage. Besides, many may think they are already doing a good job meeting the other's emotional needs, or they would have heard about it, right? Why open a can of worms that, once opened, could ruin everything?

That's a good question, and it gets to the core of why many married couples don't try to evaluate each other's effectiveness unless the situation has deteriorated significantly. They often feel that it's insensitive to try to improve their partner's skills in meeting their needs.

It will be very tough for either of you to admit that an important need is not being met as it should be. For one thing, you are trying to be as supportive and encouraging to each other as possible. Complaining is exactly the opposite of what you want to express to each other. But if you are dissatisfied with the way your partner is meeting your needs, it's important to reveal that fact now.

If you want to become skilled in anything, you must receive feedback as to how you are doing. That way you are able to correct your mistakes and improve your overall performance. Learning to become experts in meeting each other's emotional needs also requires feedback. Otherwise, there is no way for you to know if you are effective in meeting them. Without feedback, your skills will suffer.

At this point, you and your partner should have already identified your own most important emotional needs individually, and that's an essential first step. The next step will be to reveal them to each other. Once revealed, meeting each other's emotional needs will represent your goals in marriage; if you meet them for the other, you will be providing the care that you both expect in your marriage. But how will you know if you are achieving those goals? How will you know if you are meeting the needs of your spouse? How will your spouse know if your needs are being met? You should have a simple, yet sensitive, way to communicate your satisfaction or dissatisfaction with the way your important needs are being met.

To help you, individually ask yourself the following questions about each of the five most important emotional needs on your lists.

1. Are you satisfied with the way your partner is meeting this need (quality)?

If your answer is "no," how would you like your partner to meet this need? Be specific and identify positive, behavioral suggestions. On a separate sheet of paper, write the need category, and under that category, list as many *I'd love it if you would* (specific, desired behavior) statements for that need as you can (e.g., Affection: "I'd love it if you would give me a ten-second hug when you come home from work.")

If your answer is "yes," how does your partner meet this need? Be specific and identify positive ways your partner meets the need. On a separate sheet of paper, write the need category, and under that category, list as many *I love it when you* (specific, desired behavior) statements for that need as you can (e.g., Admiration: "I love it when you text me every afternoon to say something you appreciate or admire about me.").

If "yes" and "no," include both *I love it when* and *I'd love it if* statements under the need category.

2. Does your partner meet this need often enough (quantity)?

If your answer is "no," how often would you like your partner to meet this need? Be specific, again using *I'd love it if* statements under the need category.

If your answer is "yes," be specific, writing down *I love it when* statements under the need category.

Action Step:

1. On a sheet of paper, privately list your top five emotional needs, leaving spaces between each need. If you need help with the ranking process, a variation is to make notecards with single words of your choice that represent each of the 10 needs listed in the previous chapters, and place them in order of importance to you; remember that these needs are associated with your romantic feeling toward your partner (e.g., Affection, Sex, Family, Money, Chores, Honesty, Looks, Activities, Talking, Admiration).

2. Under each category listed, identify as many *I'd love it if you would* (specific, desired behavior) and *I love it when you*

(specific, desired behavior) statements as you can (see below for ideas), using a separate sheet of paper if needed.

I'd Love It If (When) Examples

Please notice that these are behaviors that make a *person happy*, not behaviors that prevent a person from feeling bad (those would go under Love Busters, not emotional needs).

Admiration: *I'd love it if you would*...give me 3 things you appreciate about me each day and vary the categories (looks, parenting, work, character, thoughtfulness); use hyperbole when telling me something you like about me, like *wow, great job* and *that was terrific when you...*; text me once a day something you appreciate about me; use *I'd love it ifs* with a positive and specific behavior to give me ideas to become more admirable.

Affection: *I'd love it if you would*...give me a kiss in the morning and say, *I love you*; use terms of endearment like *sweetie* and *honey*; text me once a day and ask how am I doing; come directly to me and give me a 10-second full-body hug and say, *I love you*  *honey* when you come home from work; give me a special card, dozen roses, a low-cost thoughtful gift, and special dinner out for special occasions like birthday, anniversary; put your arm around me or hold my hand for at least 10 minutes when we are at church or a movie; open the door for me and hold my hand for a minute when out doing errands; when you are getting yourself something, like a glass of water or a snack, you would ask me if I would like that as well.

Intimate Conversation: *I'd love it if you would*...call me in the morning, lunchtime, and afternoon and ask me about my day and tell me about yours; read the newspaper for __ minutes a day and bring up 3 interesting news ideas you found (talking about humanitarian and political world issues are my favorite); read a book with me that we both enjoy and discuss what we liked after reading; go for a walk after dinner to talk about the day.

Domestic Support: *I'd love it if you would*...schedule the kids' doctor/dentist appointments; spend time before I come home from work to put the kids' toys in a basket; keep the kitchen countertop free from clutter; do these domestic tasks: _____...that we share in the responsibility, but it makes me feel really happy when you do them; spend 1 hour each Saturday organizing and de-cluttering; make a family dinner __ times each week; take cooking classes with me (this could also be a Recreational Companionship activity); when you see something that needs to be done around the house, like replenishing the bar of soap in the shower or taking out the full garbage to the outside garbage pail, you would do it at that time.

Honesty and Openness: *I'd love it if you would*...spend 15 minutes each night on the sofa and tell me 1) a good thing/bad thing about your day, 2) your schedule for tomorrow, 3) ideas for our 15 hours together, and 4) something you appreciate about me or are thankful for; use a 1-5 rating scale (5 being great) when I ask you how you feel about an idea and, even better, after the number give me 2 sentences of why you feel that way; use *I'd love it ifs* to let me know if you are unhappy about something; say *let's negotiate* if you are not happy with a decision option; on a date, answer one E^2: *Explore and Engage* app question with me (mobile app available for Apple and Android).

Family Commitment: *I'd love it if you would*...pray with the kids before bedtime and read a Bible story; be home for family dinners each night; come up with 3 ideas for a family weekend activity and we would choose the final option together; at dinner, ask the kids their good thing/bad thing about the day; spend individual time with each child every week to ask how they are doing at school, any problems with friends, and tell them something you admire about them in their character or values; lead a family worship time each week; help the children memorize Bible verses.

Financial Support: *I'd love it if you would*...spend 15 minutes each Saturday to review our budget situation; complete a budget together; finish college to improve your career options; find a job that allowed you to be home every night; find a job that would pay for our household "needs" and my income would go to the "wants"; negotiate our wants together; pay our bills and give me an update once a month.

Physical Attractiveness: *I'd love it if you would*...run with me each morning; let me pick out the clothes in your closet that I love for dates and pick out the clothes that I really don't like (to be given away); take a shower before bed; put makeup and lipstick on before I come home from work; wear jeans, skirt, or pants around the house (no sweat pants please); wear high heels when we are on a special date; have your hair colored and/or cut once/month; have a manicure/pedicure 1/week; create a schedule for exercise each week; ask me before changing your hairstyle; wear cologne (perfume) when out on a date and the weekends.

Recreational Companionship: *I'd love it if you would*...schedule __ times per week where we go out and do something together that we both enjoy; play video games with me for 1/2 hour a night; take golf lessons with me 1/week so we could play 18 holes together 1/month; identify 5 activities we both enjoy, and schedule at least 1 recreational activity every Saturday.

Sexual Fulfillment: *I'd love it if you would*...tell me what makes our time of intimacy more enjoyable for you; schedule times for intimacy with me when you have the most energy in the day, about __ times/week; take __ minutes to cuddle in bed together after sex.

Take a Second Look

After reading the following additional instructions, *individually* review your emotional needs list a second time for accuracy of your ranking and clarity of your positive, behavioral suggestions.

1. Review: An emotional need is a **craving** that, when satisfied, leaves you with a feeling of happiness and contentment, and when unsatisfied, leaves you with the feeling of unhappiness and frustration.

2. Does your list identify your *current* top five needs that give you the most pleasure when you have it met and creates the most frustration when you don't have it met? Have you ranked them 1 to 5? Did you, imagine that you could only have one need met, and is that your #1 emotional need? If you could only have one more need, is that your #2 emotional need? Does this list represent the needs that, when met by your partner, would make you the happiest?

3. When you are finished, look over your ranking one more time. Ask yourself these questions:

   o If your partner meets all five needs you have listed, would you be happy?

   o Do you think having those needs met would sustain your feeling of love?

   o If your partner fails to meet a need, not on your list, would it threaten your feeling of love? If there is a 6th need that you feel must be included to ensure that your feeling would be sustained, add it to the list. But then allow your partner to also add a sixth need to his or her list.

4. The Action Step asked you to identify specific ways that each of your top five emotional needs could be better satisfied in your relationship. For example, if affection is ranked in the top five, you may write, "I'd love it if you would put your arm around me when we watch TV, go to a movie, or go to church." Describe what you want (quality) and how often you want it (quantity). Did you use a separate sheet of paper for this listing? Are your suggestions specific and offer a positive, desired behavior?

After you have carefully identified your ranked emotional needs and specific suggestions for meeting them, you may schedule a time to exchange your lists with your partner (The Action Step in chapter Eleven will offer some guidance). The feedback you receive will help you become an expert at giving the gift of care.

Thought Questions

1. What problems may arise when you try to communicate the need for improvement in meeting emotional needs?

2. Do you now know how to do this without risking hurt feelings or do you have a better way to be honest? Reminder: One way is to be prepared by first writing down what your partner already does that meets that need in an "I love it when you (specific, desired behavior)" statement, and then identifying suggestions that could meet your needs that are in the form of an "I'd love it if (specific, desired behavior)." Also, remember that people usually like hearing positive behaviors versus negative behaviors...avoiding statements with a "not," like *I'd love it if you wouldn't.*

9

Listening and Responding

There is an important similarity between growing as a thoughtful spouse and growing as Christ's disciple: To put it simply, they both require a lifestyle that respectfully *listens* and thoughtfully *responds*.

To become a thoughtful spouse, it takes listening to your husband or wife and creating a lifestyle in response to what is heard. You listen to your spouse and respond by making habit adjustments. The purpose of this book is to help you become a more thoughtful spouse.

To be growing as a follower of Jesus, or becoming more Christ-like, it takes listening to God and striving to create a lifestyle in response that shows His Kingship. In fact, our listening and responding to Him is the true mark of those in a relationship with Him.

In the chapters to come, you will be given opportunities to listen and thoughtfully respond to your spouse; but God also speaks to those who will listen. And His clearest revelation was through the Son, Jesus of Nazareth. In fact, if you want to listen to Him speak, listen to the words of Jesus Christ.

The Wedding Feast

Jesus told a story about a wedding celebration that a king was preparing for his son (Matthew 22: 1-14). The king sent out his servants to bring the invited guests. But they refused to come.

> [8] Then he said to his servants, 'The wedding feast is ready, but those invited were not worthy. [9] Go therefore to

the main roads and invite to the wedding feast as many as you find.' [10] And those servants went out into the roads and gathered all whom they found, both bad and good. So the wedding hall was filled with guests.

[11] "But when the king came in to look at the guests, he saw there a man who had no wedding garment. [12] And he said to him, 'Friend, how did you get in here without a wedding garment?' And he was speechless. [13] Then the king said to the attendants, 'Bind him hand and foot and cast him into the outer darkness. In that place there will be weeping and gnashing of teeth.'

In this story, the king promised a banquet for the "bad and good" people who accepted his invitation. The door to the feast was wide open. But one guest who came did not wear a wedding garment. His failure caused him to be thrown out. The ones who came and wore wedding garments were able to enjoy an elaborate celebration of the king; a feast of undeserved gifts in his presence.

Jesus' parable was referring to the Kingdom of God. From this, we have a *glimpse* that the Kingdom of God has an open door; an open invitation to all. It is filled with blessings, abundant and unimaginable. But what does the part about the man being thrown out for not wearing the right *wedding garment* symbolize? And how can we make sure we have the *wedding garment* needed?

Many Biblical scholars have helped answer these questions, but John Calvin wrote clearly: "As to the wedding garment, is it faith, or is it a holy life? This is a useless controversy; for faith cannot be separated from good works, nor do good works proceed from any other source than from faith." He then goes on to basically say that this is about the *call* for us to be renewed, taking off our old self and putting on the new self that comes through our faith in Christ Jesus (Colossians 3:9; Ephesians 4:22); to "lead a new life, that the garment [wedding clothing] may correspond to so honorable a calling."[1]

No follower of Jesus can claim perfection in leading this new life worthy of the King. *Thankfully,* that is *not* a prerequisite for God's Kingdom. When you put your faith in all that God, through Jesus Christ, has done for you, you receive unimaginable, incredible gifts. And one gift is the presence of His Holy Spirit that allows us to listen and thoughtfully respond to Him in ways that are impossible on our own (Ezekiel 36:26-27, John 14:26, Romans 8:26).

Remember Zacchaeus? He clearly understood what was needed. He accepted Jesus' invitation and declared Him as Lord. As a result, he started to listen and respond; he acknowledged his self-serving behavior and made God-honoring lifestyle adjustments.

Do you have a relationship with God? Have you accepted Christ's invitation? If you have, are you listening and responding to Him? Are you making lifestyle adjustments that reflect His Kingship in your life?

The Kingdom of God is here and now! God wants a personal, dynamic relationship with you here and now—imperfections and all. And you can receive this invitation and enjoy God's promises today and forever. Just as He called Zacchaeus nearly 2000 years ago, He *calls you* by name and wants to give and receive gifts of love with you, too!

Thought Questions

1. Are you in a relationship with God? If you're not sure, you can be sure right now! Receive Jesus Christ's invitation, and

---

[1] John Calvin. "Commentary on Matthew 22" (Verse 11). *Calvin's Commentary on the Bible*. Retrieved from www.studylight.org/commentaries/cal/matthew-22.html.

then listen and respond to His guidance. Remember, it's not about saying the right words—it's what's in your heart. But if you are searching for what to say, here's a suggestion:

Dear Jesus,

I accept your invitation to enter into Your Kingdom. I know I'm not worthy because my sinful life has separated me from You. But I believe that You died for my sins, and through Your death and resurrection, I can be forgiven. With your help, I want to turn away from my self-serving life and exchange it for a life that pleases You. I want to start listening and responding to You by learning about the life You want me to lead and then make lifestyle changes that reflect Your will.

If you entered into a relationship with God at this time, please tell your partner. Luke 15:7 says there's "joy in heaven" right NOW, but there's *also* rejoicing on earth with your *brothers* and *sisters*!

2. If you are already in a relationship with God, have you told anyone about this gift lately? If the answer is "no," tell one person this week about your relationship. This gift is to be shared!

10
Fine-tuning the Gift of Care

H ave you ever listened to someone play an out-of-tune violin? When our teenage daughter was becoming a skilled violinist, her performance would be ear-piercing if she didn't first tune the strings with a tuning fork. We rely on a tuning fork because we are unable to find that perfect pitch without it. And when the strings are perfectly tuned, playing and listening are both enjoyable.

In the next chapter, you and your partner will be giving and receiving a "tuning fork"; you will share the valuable information about the emotional needs with each other. If you're aware of specific ways to meet your spouse's most important emotional needs, then you can "fine-tune" your habits to become an expert at meeting those needs. This fine-tuning process is an essential part of caring—and it's an essential part in sustaining your spouse's feeling of romantic love for you.

But now, let's discuss another tuning fork—identifying what pleases God. If you are aware of what pleases Him, then you can fine-tune your habits to give Him your gift of care.

How Can We Give God the Gift of Care

Remember—the gift of care is defined as a willingness and effort to do what you can to make the other happy—being a source of happiness or pleasure. But can we actually make God happy with our behaviors? According to the Bible, we certainly can! It's filled with examples of how a person's behavior "pleased" or gives "pleasure" to God (1 Kings 3:10, 1 Chronicles 29:17, Psalm 147:11,

Psalm 149:4, Philippians 2:13, Hebrews 11:5, 13:16). And what pleased God in all of these instances was to create a lifestyle of *doing* His will because of our faith in Him.

More specifically, He wants us to:

1. respect and honor Him
2. love Him with all of our being
3. love and care for others

These three areas are emphasized throughout the Bible, and should come as no surprise to any believer. When we do them, God is pleased, and when we don't, He is displeased.

If you want to learn more about these three areas of God's will and more, we encourage you to read our book *Let's Get Growing, Christians!* (Harley/Chalmers, 2003). It will help you understand the will of God for your life. But at this time, I'd like you to think about only one of these ways to please Him—His desire for us to love and care for others.

God wants you to care for others, but He's given you one person to love and care for in a very special way—your spouse. When you marry, you promise to give your spouse your very best care. And you make that promise not only to your spouse, but to God as well. You promise to care for this special person for the rest of your life.

When you fulfill that promise to God, it pleases Him—It makes Him happy. In other words, one way you can give God the gift of care is by loving and caring for your spouse.

Caring for Your Spouse ... One Way to Give God the Gift of Care

If you commit your life to pleasing God, in effect, you are committing your life to the care of others. This was the essence of Christ's teaching when He said, "'Love the Lord your God with all your heart and with all your soul and with all your mind.' This is the first and greatest commandment. And the second is like it: 'Love your neighbor as yourself'" (Matthew 22:37-39 NIV).

Scripture clearly defines a follower of Christ's responsibility: To care for people whether they are friends or enemies. The reason is easy to understand: He is the authority on love. John 3:16 says, "For God so loved the world, that he gave his only Son, that whoever believes in Him should not perish but have eternal life."

So if we love God, we will take good care of our neighbor because it pleases Him. And as we already identified your closest "neighbor," and one person most affected by your actions is your partner.

Within marriage, you have a unique opportunity to provide exceptional care. God could have made us solely dependent on Him to meet all our emotional needs. But He didn't. Instead, He delegated this important job of meeting particular emotional needs to the unique relationship of marriage.

We can give God the gift of care by doing God's will in our daily lives—worshiping and loving Him, and loving others. When it comes to loving others, your relationship with your spouse is a high priority for God.

> With God, our gifts of love are not a means to the relationship, but a result of it.

When you create habits to meet your spouse's most important emotional needs, you will be using a "tuning fork" that not only gives the gift of care to your spouse but to God as well.

By fine-tuning your life to meet your spouse's emotional needs, you give the gift of care to both your spouse and to God at the same time. You avoid the ear-piercing sound that comes from a life that is out of tune and create a sweet melody that comes from a caring relationship.

P.S. We have a unique opportunity—to have a personal relationship with our Creator, God. But here's a reminder about this relationship: Don't confuse caring for your spouse and doing God-pleasing habits as the way to "earn" this relationship. It's not how you live your life—it's how Christ lived His. Without His death and resurrection, and your faith in Him, *every* caring act is worthless in God's sight.

In Romans 3, Paul gives us this reminder, "for all have sinned and fall short of the glory of God" (vs. 23) and "...no one does good, not even one" (vs. 12). But through God's grace and our faith, we can enter into a relationship with Him without having done anything good enough to deserve it. In Hebrews 11:6 it says, "And without faith it is impossible to please him, for whoever would draw near to God must believe that he exists and that he rewards those who seek him." Our gifts of love to God are not a means to the relationship, but a result of our faith that He is ALL that He is.

Thought Questions

1. Will the behaviors you want to create in your relationship with God automatically turn into habits simply because you're a Christian or you "will" it to happen? The answer is "no." So, here's a suggestion: For the next four weeks, create three new behaviors that you will review daily. Review, practice, and prayer will make sure these behaviors become habits!

2. Would you say that living in God's will is easy? If you are struggling with one of the areas above, here are some steps you can take to help you live according to God's will.

Steps to Solving Spiritual Problems
(From *Let's Get Growing, Christians!* Harley/Chalmers, 2003)

> ➤ Pray daily for a solution to the problem
> ➤ Have faith that, between you and God, it can be solved
> ➤ Think of ways the problem could be solved
> ➤ Put your best plan into action

Remember: John wrote, "This is the confidence we have in approaching God: that if we ask anything according to His will, He hears us. And if we know that He hears us—whatever we ask—we know that we have what we asked of Him" (1 John 5:14-15 NIV).

11

Becoming an Expert at Care

After Dennis and Mary learned about their own needs and identified specific suggestions for how each need could be met, they made a trade. Mary agreed to start meeting Dennis's top five emotional needs and Dennis agreed to meet Mary's needs. This was so important to them that they even wrote down and signed their commitment.

At first, it all seemed too "prescribed" for Mary, as if Dennis was simply following the agreement without being genuine. "Is this how it's going to feel for the rest of our marriage?" she thought. But she reminded herself about what they learned: "It takes time for behavior to become habits, and at first they may seem awkward," and "As needs are met, love units are deposited and eventually romantic love is restored." The good thing was that she and Dennis were daily trying to get into the habit of caring for each other, something they had once done so effortlessly.

As days passed and her efforts were more consistent, she noticed that it was getting easier to meet Dennis's emotional needs. She also noticed that Dennis was more at ease with caring for her. They weren't "there" yet, but definitely on their way to creating a new lifestyle of care.

Agree to Meet Each Other's Needs

It's assumed that a husband and wife will care for each other, but because most marital agreements or wedding vows are so vague, they often fail to specify the care that is needed. That's why I suggest that couples come to a formal understanding with each other.

To help clarify this understanding, I have provided the Marital Promise for you and your spouse to complete. There are spaces in the agreement to name the emotional needs identified as most important to each of you.

Action Step: Schedule 30-45 minutes with your partner (as soon as you are both prepared) which will give you an opportunity to gather information about your partner's top five (or six) most important emotional needs and specific behavioral suggestions to improve your need-meeting skills.

But before you meet, make sure the following is prepared, asking yourself these questions:

- Have I identified my top five most important emotional needs?

- Do I have specific behavioral suggestions to offer my partner on how those needs could be met?

- Are they in the form of "I'd love it if (specific, positive behavior)" and "I love it when"? Are they written down?

- Am I ready to gather information so I can be more effective in meeting my partner's most important emotional needs?

When you meet, ask your partner to identify what may be his or her top five (or six) emotional needs at this point in time, and gather one to four *I'd love it ifs* and *I love it whens*, with specific, desired behavior, to help you understand how each need could be met, if mutually agreeable. This action step is about listening and gathering information; it is not about identifying whether or not will do the behavior.

If you need any help with this Action Step, or if either partner is behaving in a way that causes love unit withdrawals, please stop and you may want to consider taking the Four Gifts of Love® Class for more guidance and encouragement for completing the action steps (www.FourGiftsofLove.Org/four-gifts-of-love-class).

It would be wise to review your emotional needs every year of your marriage, because needs may change over time. In some years, the change may not be very great—perhaps just a reordering of needs. But for example, in the year a couple has their first child, new needs may completely replace some of the old ones. In these situations, couples must remind themselves that *care* means meeting each other's most important emotional needs, even when those needs change during a lifetime together. And to know what they are, you will need to check with each other regularly.

Becoming an Expert at Care

Your partner's honesty about how well you are meeting his or her needs considers two aspects of care—quality and quantity. Quality refers to meeting the need in a way that is satisfying—it deals with the manner in which you go about meeting a need. For example, in meeting the need for conversation, you must learn how to make the conversation enjoyable for your partner. You are not actually meeting a need unless the quality of your care meets your partner's minimum standards.

Quantity refers to meeting the need often enough—it deals with how often and how long you spend meeting a need. Some people don't require fulfillment very often, while others want it frequently. Intimate conversation is one of those needs that, for some, may be satisfied with a short chat a few times a week, and for others, may require conversations for longer periods of time and more often.

As you learn to meet each other's emotional needs, you should satisfy both the quality and quantity requirements to make your partner happy. Quantity is fairly easy to understand, because your partner will tell you how often and how much he or she wants the need met.

Quality is more difficult to communicate. Sometimes even the one with the need doesn't understand exactly what's missing when the quality isn't quite there. If you know that quality improvements are needed but you are at a loss to know how to make them, I suggest that you read Dr. Harley's book, *His Needs, Her Needs: Making Romantic Love Last* (Harley, 1986, 2022) and its accompanying workbook, *Five Steps to Romantic Love* (Harley, 2002, 2012). These books will help you think through each need and give you more ideas as to how they can be met to each other's satisfaction. In addition, to help you remember your own plan to meet your spouse's needs, you may want to download and use T*he Gift of Care* mobile app from FourGiftsofLove.org, Google Play, and Apple App Store.

Improve Your Skills: Meet Each Other's Needs in Ways that Are Mutually Enjoyable

Since you have given each other the exclusive right to meet some of each other's most important emotional needs (such as sexual fulfillment), as a spouse, you have an obligation to meet them for each other. There are no other ethical alternatives. But if you don't enjoy meeting them for each other, you risk making Love Bank withdrawals whenever you try. And you also risk developing an aversive reaction to meeting that need.

You already know how you can make Love Bank withdrawals—you do it whenever you associate your partner with a bad experience. But you may not know what an aversive reaction is. Let me explain.

Psychologists have known for years that if you do something unpleasant for long enough, your emotions will react very negatively whenever you think about it. In anticipation of doing it yet again, you may have a headache, feel dizzy, or even feel so sick that you cannot keep food down. I've counseled many who feel that way whenever they try to make love with their spouse because their past lovemaking experiences have been so unpleasant for them.

Being in love can tempt people to meet each other's important emotional needs at all costs. They try to appear interested in their spouse's conversation, even when the subject is very boring to them. They try to enjoy recreational activities that their spouse enjoys. And they try to make love in ways that please their spouse, even if they are humiliated, or worse, experiencing pain. But I strongly advise everyone to avoid doing this.

> You should both agree to meet each other's needs only in ways that are enjoyable for both of you. Never expect the other person to suffer or sacrifice so that your emotional need can be met.

The care you show each other should be mutual care. You should both agree to meet each other's needs only in ways that are enjoyable for both of you. Never expect the other person to suffer or sacrifice so that your emotional need can be met.

There is a great deal of wisdom behind this recommendation. The most important reason for avoiding sacrifice (i.e., pain/suffering) is that you care for each other, and that means neither of you should want the other one to suffer. How much gratification can you receive knowing that your spouse is unhappy in the way he or she is meeting one of your needs? In fact, most needs are best met only when your partner enjoys meeting them for you.

If your spouse is bored by a particular topic of conversation but knows that you like to talk about it for hours, how can you possibly be fulfilled by the conversation, knowing that he or she is very uncomfortable? The same is true for recreational companionship. Is it fun to engage in an activity with someone who would rather be somewhere else?

Sex is particularly sensitive to mutual enjoyment. If one spouse forces himself or herself into having sex as often as needed, does that make it fulfilling? I've counseled many wives who agreed to have sex as often as requested, and their husband leaves every experience fuming. Why? It's because she was so unhappy while trying to make love to him. The only way he can be sexually fulfilled is if she enjoys making love too.

But there are other reasons to avoid sacrificing your own feelings to meet an emotional need. As I just mentioned, when you don't enjoy meeting your partner's emotional need, you make Love Bank withdrawals every time you try. Your partner's gain is your loss. You lose love for your partner every time you try to fulfill the need.

And then there's also the problem of aversive reactions. Unless you enjoy meeting your partner's emotional needs, you risk becoming emotionally upset or even physically ill whenever you try. Eventually, it will seem impossible to meet those needs that are so important in marriage.

As you already know, I want you to meet each other's important emotional needs as often as you want them to be met. I want spouses to be affectionate with each other every day, to talk to each other regularly with depth and understanding, to be each other's favorite recreational companions, and to make love to each other often. If you are to achieve those objectives, you must work together to find ways to meet those needs in a *mutually* enjoyable way.

The way you meet your spouse's needs must take your own feelings into account as well as the feelings of your spouse. If you are to be a skilled conversationalist, you must pick topics that interest you as much as they interest your spouse. Your recreational activities must be enjoyable to you as well as to him or her. And whenever you make love, the skills you develop must enable both of you to enjoy the sexual experience. To repeatedly suffer while meeting your spouse's emotional needs will not only fail to satisfy him or her, but it will also threaten your love for each other. And it may create such a strong aversive reaction that you eventually fail to meet your spouse's need entirely.

The more you enjoy doing something, the more often you will do it. The less you enjoy something, the less you will do it. If you and your partner want to meet each other's needs often and with enthusiasm, you must create an experience you both enjoy. This will ensure that your needs will be met with regularity and consistency. And when that happens, you'll be keeping your promise to care for each other for the rest of your lives.

Thought Questions

1. Will the behaviors listed on your spouse's sheet turn into habits simply because you want it to happen? (The answer is "no.")

2. What must happen to make a behavior become a habit? (Remember, you must practice a behavior before it becomes a habit. *The Gift of Care* mobile app from FourGiftsofLove.org, Google Play, and Apple App Store could help you remember your spouse's most important emotional needs.)

✿ Talk About This

Reminder: Please keep the conversation **BRIEF** and **STAY ON** the topic of the questions. And most importantly, use this time to practice your gifts of care and protection, being especially careful to avoid disrespectful comments. Remember, your goals are to be a source of happiness and avoid being a source of pain in your relationship.

1. In chapter Seven, the topic of exclusive need meeting was discussed. Since this topic is SO important, here is an excerpt from the reading for your review together:

    "But a word of caution: If a need is so important to you that you're likely to fall in love with the one who meets it, that need should be met exclusively in marriage. Why? Because if someone of the opposite sex meets that need, you are at risk of having an affair—one of the worst ways to betray your spouse. When you marry, you should give each other an exclusive right to meet your most important intimate emotional needs so you will love each other exclusively.

    "This exclusive right to meet each other's important intimate emotional needs places responsibility on your shoulders to meet those needs. After all, if your spouse promises not to let anyone else meet those needs, and then you fail to meet them yourself, your spouse will be in a very unpleasant and frustrating situation.

    "Sexual fulfillment is one of the more obvious intimate emotional needs that should be met exclusively in marriage, but there are others that can be just as significant. For example, an affair doesn't usually begin with sex; it begins with the most intimate form of conversation, where personal feelings and problems are shared. If conversation can cause you to fall in love with someone of the opposite sex, your most intimate conversation should be limited to your spouse. The same is true of affection and recreational companionship. If you let someone other than your spouse meet those needs, you'll risk having an affair – one of the worst mistakes you could ever make in life."

2. With what you have learned so far about the Love Bank and the most important emotional needs, what would happen if you allow someone else of the opposite gender to meet your most important emotional needs? How would that affect that person's account in your Love Bank?

3. What lifestyle rules could a couple follow to make it difficult for someone of the opposite gender to make enough deposits into their Love Banks to trigger the feeling of romantic love for that person? How can you protect your Love Banks from outside threats?

PART TWO

The Gift of Protection

I PROMISE TO AVOID
BEING THE CAUSE
OF YOUR UNHAPPINESS

12

The Gift of Protection with God

You and your partner are very capable of hurting each other. In fact, if you're not careful, you can become each other's greatest source of unhappiness. So to avoid that tragic outcome, Part Two will help you both learn how to give the gift of protection.

God also wants us to give Him the gift of protection—a willingness and effort to avoid being a source of His unhappiness. God can be very offended by the way we treat Him and others, and He tries to communicate what makes Him unhappy in "commands" that are found in His word.

Unfortunately, many are turned off by the concept of "rules" or "commands." They don't want to be told what to do. But if they were to take the time to look at each one of God's "rules," they would notice something very surprising—by following His commands, they not only avoid being the source of displeasure to God, they avoid being the source of pain to themselves and others. Giving this gift to God spares everyone from the devastating consequences of failing to follow His wisdom.

Anyone who has been on the receiving end of a broken rule of God knows how much suffering it can cause themselves and others around them. About 90% of the people I counsel are trying to recover from infidelity. Most betrayed spouses consider this betrayal to be the most painful experience of their lives. Everyone suffers: the children, wayward spouse, and lover. Without a doubt, adultery causes unhappiness. And God knew it would turn out that way!

When God gave us the Ten Commandments (Exodus 20:1-17) or when Jesus told us about the New Commandments (Matthew 22:37-39), He was not trying to control or enslave us. He was trying to protect us and others from the inevitable pain and suffering that comes from a thoughtless life. Paul reminded the Galatians of this fact when he said, "For freedom Christ has set us free; stand firm therefore, and do not submit again to a yoke of slavery [to sin]" (Galatians 5:1). As any loving father would do, He gives us rules of life that lead to less suffering and greater happiness.

But His rules also help us avoid causing Him to grieve. In Ephesians 4:30-32 it says, "And do not grieve the Holy Spirit of God, by whom you were sealed for the day of redemption. Let all bitterness and wrath and anger and clamor and slander be put away from you, along with all malice. Be kind to one another, tenderhearted, forgiving one another, as God in Christ forgave you." In other words, when we strive to create a lifestyle that follows His rules, we are showing a willingness and effort to avoid being the cause of His unhappiness—giving Him our gift of protection.

Action Step: On a sheet of paper, list your habits that cause God to be unhappy. Spend time in prayer asking Him to reveal these habits. Then identify a list of specific alternative behavior(s) to replace the undesirable behavior. To help you with this replacement, you may want to memorize verses to support your new behavior and avoidance of the old habit. (The concordance section of your Bible could help you find these verses.) You may want to write the verses on a note card and carry them around with you until they are memorized.

Example

a. Quickly becoming angry with others when I hear something that upsets me

b. Take time to listen and don't respond until I can restate in my mind or aloud what I heard. If what I heard was upsetting, ask to be excused for a moment, and calm down until I can speak with care and control.

c. James 1:19-20—Know this, my beloved brothers: let every person be quick to hear, slow to speak, slow to anger; for the anger of man does not produce the righteousness of God.

Review daily for the next four weeks. Then continue your review on the 1st of every month. Pray daily for God's help as you develop these new behaviors. "Commit your work to the Lord, and your plans will be established" (Proverbs 16:3).

Thought Questions

1. Do you know someone who has consistently obeyed all of God's commands? If you think someone qualifies, you don't know that person well enough. That's because *no one* is totally consistent in obeying His commands: "For all have sinned and fall short of the glory of God" (Romans 3:23). And yet, God requires complete obedience.

2. So how can we be in a relationship with God if it's impossible to obey Him completely? The answer is found in the verses that follow the one cited above: We, sinners, "are justified by his grace as a gift, through the redemption that is in Christ Jesus, whom God put forward as a propitiation [a sacrifice necessary to be made right with God] by his blood, to be received by faith" (Romans 3:24-25a). And that faith makes us His children: "But to all who did receive him, who believed in his name, he gave the right to become children of God" (John 1:12).

13
What Is Protection, Part I

I f you love each other today, it's the result of doing a good job caring for each other: Meeting each other's emotional needs. You have deposited so many love units in each other's Love Bank that your balances have broken through the romantic love threshold.

But all those love units that you've carefully deposited could quickly be withdrawn. That's because you not only can make each other very happy, but you can also make each other very unhappy.

I know you don't want to hurt each other. Yet if you are not careful, you can become the greatest source of each other's unhappiness. And if you don't make a special effort to protect each other from your selfish instincts, that unhappiness is inevitable.

You may have already discovered how easy it is to offend each other. From what you've learned, you have probably made a special effort to avoid being inconsiderate. For example, you may already be asking how your partner feels about something you're planning, because you've learned that almost everything you do affects him or her.

Quite frankly, if you had not learned to be thoughtful to each other during courtship, you probably wouldn't have considered marriage. Inconsiderate behavior withdraws so many love units that couples who indulge in it don't stay in love very long. Your care for each other's emotional needs created your love, but it's been your thoughtfulness that has kept your love alive. Will you continue to be as considerate after marriage?

To help you remember to be considerate of each other's feelings for the rest of your lives, I suggest that you give each other the second gift of love, Protection: a willingness and effort to do what you can to avoid making the other unhappy—to avoid being a source of unhappiness. Essentially, it is a promise to stop being a source of your spouse's unhappiness and do whatever it takes to avoid destructive tendencies for your spouse's protection. This gift guards you from selfish tendencies that tempt you to gain at each other's expense, or worse yet, to deliberately try to hurt each other.

> When you meet each other's most important emotional needs, you become each other's source of greatest *happiness*. But if you are not careful, you can also become each other's source of greatest *unhappiness*.

When you meet each other's most important emotional needs, you become each other's source of greatest *happiness*. But if you are not careful, you can also become each other's source of greatest *unhappiness*.

Love Busters: Habits that Destroy Romantic Love

Whenever you do anything that makes your partner unhappy, you withdraw some love units. Each careless act takes something away from the love you have for each other. But most of what we do doesn't happen only once. That's because we're creatures of habit.

Most of our behavior is in the form of habits that we repeat. If you've done anything once, it's likely that you've done it before and that you'll do it again. And if it makes your partner unhappy, you'll continue to make him or her unhappy until you change that habit.

Habits that meet each other's emotional needs help you make Love Bank deposits almost effortlessly. But habits that make the other unhappy also make withdrawals almost effortlessly. And those withdrawals can be relentless. If you repeatedly do anything that makes your partner unhappy, your Love Bank withdrawals will cancel out your deposits and threaten your love for each other. I call habits that cause repeated withdrawals *Love Busters*, because that's what they do: Destroy romantic love.

In the simplest terms, Love Busters are those things you are likely to do on a regular basis that make each other unhappy. I've learned about almost all the ways that couples can hurt each other. From the thousands of complaints I've heard, I've  been able to classify them into six categories: selfish demands, disrespectful judgments, angry outbursts, dishonesty, annoying habits, and independent behavior. If your partner has ever done, or will ever do, anything to make you unhappy, it will fall into one of these six categories. Each of them represents a type of thoughtless behavior that couples tend to repeat throughout their married life. Let's take a closer look at each of them.

Selfish Demands

Selfish demands are attempts to force your partner to do things that would benefit you at your partner's expense.

Our parents made demands on us when we were children; teachers made demands in school; and employers make demands at work. Most of us didn't like them as children, and we still don't like them now.

But when we were children, our parents' demands often made sense. If we didn't do what we were told, chaos would have reigned. When we were in school, we wouldn't have learned much had we not obeyed our teachers. And even our employers can often get away with making demands because we get paid to do what we're told.

In marriage, however, demands don't make sense. We're no longer children, we're not in school, and our spouse cannot pay us to be obedient—we already own our money jointly. But there's an even more important reason to avoid demands: You withdraw love units every time you tell your spouse what to do.

I'm sure you have both witnessed abuse in marriage. You have seen it on television, read about it in newspapers, and maybe even been a witness to one spouse's abuse of the other. I'm also sure that you want to avoid it in your marriage at all costs. So take very seriously what I say next: *Selfish demands* are the first stage of abuse in marriage.

If you demand something of your partner, you're being abusive because you're trying to force him or her to do what you want. In most cases, demands carry a threat of punishment: *If you refuse me, you'll regret it.* In other words, *You may dislike doing what I want, but if you don't do it, I'll see to it that you suffer great pain.* A demand is "an offer you can't refuse."

People who make demands don't seem to care how others feel. They think only of their own needs: *If you find it unpleasant to do what I want, tough! And if you refuse, I'll make it even tougher.*

A *request* is the right way to ask for anything from your partner. Following your request, you should ask how he or she would feel fulfilling your request: *How would you feel about* (the request)? If the response is positive—your partner would be happy to do what you ask—you're in business. But if the response is negative, or even hesitant, trying to force the issue would be a big mistake. Reluctance may be due to any number of causes—personal needs, comfort level, a sense of what's wise or fair, and so forth. But be assured that there is a reason for reluctance, and from your partner's viewpoint, it's a good reason.

If you try to force your partner to do what you want, you may get your demand now, but it makes you less likely to get it in the future. The next time it's needed, your spouse will resist you with even greater force. But even if your partner were to submit to every demand, you would withdraw love units every time. You would be getting your way at the expense of your partner's love for you. Eventually, he or she would hate you.

Sometimes a wife says, "But you don't know my husband! He lies around the house all night, and I can't get him to do a thing. The only time he lifts a finger is to press the remote-control buttons. If I don't insist that he get up and help me, nothing would get done."

"Requests don't work with my wife," a husband might say. "She only thinks about herself! She spends her whole life shopping and going out with her girlfriends. If I didn't demand that she stay at home once in a while, I'd never see her."

My answer to these common arguments is that demands are an ineffective way to get a husband to help around the house or to keep a wife from going out with her friends. Demands do not encourage people to cooperate; they only withdraw love units. If you force your partner to meet your needs, it becomes a temporary solution at best. Threats, lectures, and other forms of manipulation do not build compatibility. They build resentment.

So when you make a request and your partner expresses reluctance, what are your alternatives?

Thoughtful negotiation. Try to revise your request to accommodate the objections your partner may offer. If you respect those objections and brainstorm a way to get what you need from your partner with his or her enthusiastic agreement, you'll get it without losing your love for each other. And you're more likely to get it again the next time you need help.

If you think that care in marriage means that your partner should do whatever you say, think again. Since you've both promised to care for each other, your care should be mutual care, with neither gaining at the other's expense. That's why your requests should be made thoughtfully, with each other's feelings in mind.

It's abusive to make selfish demands. It will prevent you from receiving what you need from each other and will cause you to lose your love for each other. Selfish demands should never be tolerated in marriage. They're a Love Buster.

Alternative Behavior

Can you think of a specific, alternative behavior
to replace the following
selfish demand?

Selfish Demand: Giving your spouse a list of chores to do on Saturday saying, *You need to do these things on Saturday.*

Alternative Behavior: Ask your spouse, *I'd love it if we could get this list done on Saturday. How would you feel about doing these chores?* If your spouse is not enthusiastic about doing the list on Saturday, ask for other options or negotiate together to find a mutually enthusiastic plan (chapter Seventeen will help you with this negotiation process).

Disrespectful Judgments

Disrespectful judgments are attempts to "straighten out" your partner's attitudes, beliefs, and behavior by trying to impose your system of values, beliefs, or way of thinking on him or her through lecture, ridicule, threats, or other forceful means.

Have you ever tried to "straighten out" someone? We're all occasionally tempted to do so. We usually think we're doing that person a big favor, lifting him or her from the darkness of confusion into the light of our superior perspective. If people would only follow our advice, we assume, they could avoid many of life's pitfalls.

But if you ever try to straighten out your partner, to keep him or her from making mistakes, you are making a much bigger mistake. Your mistake withdraws love units and destroys romantic love. I call this tactic, *disrespectful judgments.*

A disrespectful judgment occurs whenever one partner tries to impose values and beliefs on the other. When one assumes that his or her own views are right and the other is woefully misguided, they enter a minefield.

The trouble starts when you think you have the right—even the responsibility—to impose your view on your partner. Almost invariably, he or she will regard such an imposition as personally threatening, arrogant, rude, and incredibly disrespectful. You then lose love units in your Love Bank account.

When you try to impose your opinions on your partner, you imply that he or she has poor judgment. That's disrespectful. You may not say it in so many words, but it's the clear message that your partner hears. It's as if you're saying, "Hey, stupid." If you value his or her judgment, you wouldn't be so quick to discard your partner's opinions. You will consider the possibility that your partner is right and you're wrong.

Disrespectful judgments is the second stage of abuse in marriage. They're abusive because they hurt your partner. They usually follow the first stage of abuse, selfish demands, because demands usually don't work. When a partner refuses to submit to a demand, force is applied by attacking his or her judgment.

Examples of disrespectful judgments are: 1) lecturing/trying to educate/giving advice without being asked; 2) implying that your opinion is superior; 3) talking over your partner or preventing him or her from having a chance to explain his or her opinion; and 4) ridiculing your partner's point of view.

Disagreement in marriage is common. But if you want to resolve your conflicts in a way that avoids Love Bank withdrawals, you should *respectfully* disagree. Try to understand your partner's perspective. Present the information that brought you to your opinion and listen to the information he or she brings. Entertain the possibility of changing your mind, instead of just trying to change your partner's mind.

That's how respectful persuasion works. You see, each of us brings two things into a marriage—wisdom and foolishness. But it can be very difficult to sort out the two. The best way to do so is to share ideas with respect, sort through the pros and cons, and eventually create an understanding that is superior to what either of you had individually. Respectful persuasion doesn't impose or force beliefs on each other. It creates consensus. And it achieves it without Love Bank withdrawals.

Disrespectful judgments, on the other hand, are the wrong way to try to persuade each other—they're abusive. If you try to get what you need from each other with disrespect, you will fail, and you'll lose your love for each other. Don't tolerate disrespectful judgments in your marriage. They're a Love Buster.

Alternative Behavior

Can you think of a specific, alternative behavior
to replace the following
disrespectful judgment?

Disrespectful Judgment: Saying, *Why did you do that? Did you really think that would solve the problem?* Or, *This is what you should have done.* Or, (with rolling eyes) *Didn't you know that was going to happen?*

Alternative Behavior: Use the phrase, *I'd love it if you would ask me for help when solving these problems;* or *Would you like some suggestions on how to solve the problem next time?*

Angry Outbursts

Angry outbursts are deliberate attempts to hurt your spouse because of anger, usually in the form of verbal or physical attacks.

What makes you angry? The feeling of anger usually occurs when we don't get what we want; we feel that someone is making us unhappy and what he or she is doing just isn't fair. In your angry state, you're convinced that reasoning won't work and the offender will keep upsetting you until he or she is taught a lesson. The only thing such people understand is punishment, you assume. Then they'll think twice about making you unhappy again!

An angry outburst offers a simple solution to your problem—punish or destroy the troublemaker. If your partner turns out to be the troublemaker, anger will urge you to hurt the very one you've promised to care for and protect. When you're angry, you don't care about his or her feelings and are willing to scorch the culprit if it helps even the score.

Angry outbursts are the third stage of abuse in marriage. When selfish demands and disrespectful judgments don't work, spouses often try to get their way with angry outbursts. These three Love Busters are the most common ingredients of a domestic fight because one almost invariably leads to the next.

Isn't it sad that a husband and wife, who promise to love and cherish each other, would revert to hurting each other in such an abusive way? It's damaging in so many ways that I hardly know where to begin in describing them all. But the most serious damage of angry outbursts is to Love Bank accounts—it's devastating.

In the end, you have nothing to gain from anger. Punishment does not solve marital problems; it only makes your partner want to inflict punishment on you—or leave you! When you become angry with your partner, you threaten his or her safety and security; you fail to provide protection. When anger wins, love loses.

Each of us has an arsenal of weapons we use when we're angry. If we think someone deserves to be punished, we unlock the gate and select an appropriate weapon. Sometimes the weapons are verbal (ridicule and sarcasm), sometimes they're devious plots to cause suffering, and sometimes they descend to the level of physical abuse. But they all have one thing in common: they are intended to hurt people. Since our partner is at such close range, we can use our weapons to hurt him or her the most.

Some of the husbands and wives I've counseled have fairly harmless arsenals, maybe just a few awkward efforts at ridicule when they're angry. Others are armed to nuclear proportions, putting their spouse's life in danger. But regardless of the danger of your angry outbursts, you should never lose your temper. You should go to extreme lengths to protect your partner from this third stage of abuse.

Anger is the most common form of insanity. If you're not convinced, have someone videotape you during your next angry outburst, and then review it when you've recovered. What you say when you're angry is not only harmful to your marriage, but it's also crazy. The best thing to do when you feel angry is to say nothing, do nothing, and try to calm down. It's only after you've regained your composure that you can address the problem that triggered your anger with wisdom. Don't try to do it while you're angry.

A wise Psalm says, "Don't sin by letting your anger control you. Think about it overnight and remain silent [*until controlled*]" (4:4 NLT).

If you can't control your temper, the problems that you and your partner face in life will accumulate. That's because anger prevents couples from addressing their conflicts constructively. Fear of an angry outburst will keep your partner from introducing issues when they are in their infancy. They will grow larger and there will be more of them if you let this Love Buster gain a foothold in your marriage.

> You can be your spouse's greatest source of pleasure, but you can also be your spouse's greatest source of pain.

Remember, you can be your spouse's greatest source of pleasure, but you can also be your spouse's greatest source of pain, particularly when he or she receives the brunt of your anger.

Angry outbursts should not be tolerated in your marriage—ever! If you find that you can't control your temper, obtain professional guidance to overcome this most destructive Love Buster. For some situations, temporary separation may be needed until safety can be assured. Having a zero-tolerance policy for angry outbursts will help protect your spouse's love for you and may even save your marriage.

Alternative Behavior

Can you think of a specific, alternative behavior
to replace the following
angry outburst?

Angry Outburst: Slamming the door when upset and refusing to speak to your spouse for days.

A Plan to Eliminate Angry Outbursts:

1. Understand: The feeling of anger usually occurs when we don't get what we want (e.g., respect, understanding, consideration, appreciation, etc.).
2. Chemicals are released into our brain and body when we don't get what we want; our fight/flight part of the brain (amygdala) is triggered.
3. Symptoms: The chemicals produce physical symptoms, like a faster heartbeat, rush or "whoosh" feeling, tight chest, hot or cold feeling, faster speech, tight jaw and forehead. When those symptoms are first felt, a person is entering irrational territory and should consider themselves a potential threat to others.
4. Remove yourself from the room: Say, "Sweety, I need to go to the bathroom. I'll be back in 5 minutes." (If in the car say, "Sweety, I need 5 minutes of quiet; then I can talk.")
5. While away, try to breathe deeper and slower and, most importantly, think of an empathetic thought because this will also help you relax. For example, "My wife/husband may have had something happen today that I don't know about that caused her/him to be late."
6. Come up with an *I'd love it if* or *I need* or *I'm not enthusiastic about that. Let's negotiate* statement. For example, "I'd love it if you would give me a text before you leave the office.
7. If you can't tell your honesty statement face-to-face, write a short note with your gift of honesty (or download and use *The Gift of Honesty* mobile app from FourGiftsofLove.org, Google Play, and Apple App Store).

Thought Questions

1. Do you agree that abuse often begins with selfish demands, escalates to disrespectful judgments, and culminates in angry outbursts?

2. The issues surrounding control and abuse are interrelated. Can you see how abuse is an effort to control? How can you safeguard your relationship against abuse?

14
What Is Protection, Part II

I n the last chapter, you learned about three Love Busters: Selfish Demands, Disrespectful Judgments, and Angry Outbursts. Now we will finish the list of Love Busters by discussing Dishonesty, Independent Behavior, and Annoying Habits.

Dishonesty

Dishonesty is a failure to reveal to your partner correct information about your thoughts, feelings, habits, likes and dislikes (emotional reactions), personal history, daily activities, and plans for the future. Dishonesty is also leaving your partner with what you know is a false impression.

Dishonesty is the strangest of the six Love Busters. No one likes dishonesty, but sometimes honesty seems more damaging. What if the truth is more painful than a lie? Should you be honest even when the truth hurts?

When a wife first learns that her husband has been unfaithful, the pain is often so great that she wishes she had been left ignorant. When a husband discovers his wife's affair, it's like a knife in his heart. *Maybe it would have been better not knowing,* he thinks. In fact, many marriage counselors advise clients to avoid telling a spouse about past infidelity, because they think it's too painful for people to handle. Besides, if it's over and done with, why dredge up the sewage of the past?

It's this sort of advice that leads some of the most well-intentioned husbands and wives to lie to each other, or at least give each other false impressions. They feel that dishonesty will help them protect their partner's feelings. But I've found that when dishonesty is discovered, the hidden behavior usually causes less pain than the dishonesty itself, even when the hidden behavior is infidelity.

This makes dishonesty a strange Love Buster. Lies clearly hurt a relationship over the long term, but truth can also hurt, especially in the short term. That's why many couples continue in dishonesty. They feel they can't take the shock of facing the truth—at least right now. As a result, the marriage dies a slow death.

But there is an important difference between the pain of a thoughtless act, such as infidelity, and the pain of being told about a thoughtless act. It isn't honesty that creates the pain—it's the thoughtless act that does the damage and the dishonesty that is usually combined with the thoughtless act. Dishonesty may defer some of that pain, but when the truth is finally revealed, the months or years of hiding it make everything worse.

Dishonesty strangles compatibility. To build compatibility, you must lay your cards on the table; you must be honest about your thoughts, feelings, habits, likes, dislikes, personal history, daily activities, and plans for the future. When misinformation is part of the mix, you have little hope of making successful adjustments to each other. Dishonesty not only makes solutions to problems hard to find, but it often leaves couples ignorant of the problems themselves.

There's another very important reason to be honest. Honesty makes our behavior more thoughtful. If we knew that everything we did and said would be televised and reviewed by all our friends, we would be far less likely to engage in thoughtless acts. Criminals would not steal and commit violent acts if they knew they would be caught each time they did. Honesty is the television camera in our lives. If we are honest about all that we do, we tend to be more thoughtful because we know those acts will be revealed—by ourselves.

In an honest relationship, thoughtless acts are revealed, corrected, and forgiven. Bad behavior is nipped in the bud before it develops into habits. Bad habits become targets for elimination.

But there's one more reason to avoid dishonesty in marriage: It hurts your partner and will destroy your love for each other if you allow it to penetrate your relationship. For that reason alone, it should not be tolerated. It's a Love Buster.

Alternative Behavior

Can you think of a specific, alternative behavior
to replace the following
dishonest behavior?

Dishonesty: 1) Keeping feelings hidden; or 2) saying "ok" to something you don't really like.

Alternative Behavior: 1) Use the phrase, *I'm bothered when you* (specific behavior). *I'd love it if next time you would* (specific, positive behavior); 2) give a rating on a scale of 1-5 (5 being the best) about a decision, then use an *I'd love it if* to offer another option: *That idea feels like a ___ (insert number rating) to me. I'd love it if we could* (specific, positive behavior); or 3) Use the phrase, *I'm not enthusiastic about that idea. Can we negotiate another option?* These are also three skills to help you be more emotionally honest (you will learn about this in chapter Twenty-one).

Annoying Habits

Annoying habits are repeated behaviors that unintentionally cause your partner to be unhappy.

When was the last time your partner did something that annoyed you? Last week? Yesterday? An hour ago? Maybe your partner is humming that irritating tune this very minute!

One of the most annoying things about annoying habits is that they don't seem all that important—but they still drive you bananas! It's not abuse or even disrespect, just annoyance. You should be able to shrug it off, but you can't. It's like the steady *drip, drip* of a leaking faucet. Annoying habits will nickel and dime your Love Bank into bankruptcy.

When we're annoyed, others seem inconsiderate, particularly when we've explained that their behavior bothers us and they continue to do it. It's not just the behavior itself, but the thought behind it—the idea that they just don't care enough to stop annoying you.

But when our behavior annoys others, we have an entirely different perspective. *It's just a little thing; why make a federal case out of it? Why can't other people adjust?*

The problem is the lack of empathy. We don't feel what others feel. As a counselor, I try to help couples become more empathetic, to try to see through each other's eyes. If they could only know what it feels like to experience their own annoying behavior, they would put more effort into changing those habits.

Annoying habits are repeated without much thought. They include personal mannerisms, such as the way you eat, the way you clean up after yourself (or don't!), and the way you talk.

Every annoying habit will drive a wedge between you and your partner, creating and sustaining incompatibility. If you want compatibility in your marriage, and you want to avoid squandering love units, you should create a plan to get rid of as many of them as you can.

Your plan should begin with a list to identify annoying habits that are doing the most damage. From that list, you should pick the three that are the most annoying. The best way to eliminate those habits is to create new non-annoying habits to replace them. And remember, you form a new habit by repeating it until you do it effortlessly. If your eating habits annoy your partner, you must practice new, acceptable eating behavior whenever you eat, whether you are together or not. Eventually, your new eating habits that please your partner will be so natural that you will never give them a thought. And instead of withdrawing love units when you eat together, you will deposit them.

Some people feel that their habits are a part of their identity. But it doesn't take much thought to see the flaw in that belief. Truth is, our habits are changing throughout our lives, while our identity stays the same. We develop a host of new skills to become successful in achieving important objectives without changing our identity one single bit. So habits that make us less annoying not only preserve Love Bank balances, but they make us more generally acceptable in a host of other situations as well.

Having operated a dating service in the past, I'm aware of the rough edges that many people have going into marriage. But within one year of marriage, I've witnessed both men and women looking and behaving much sharper, largely because they have responded positively to each other's suggestions for improvement. And many of those suggestions involve habits that were annoying before marriage.

If you find that the list of annoying habits she makes is much longer than the one he makes, don't be surprised. I've found that, in general, women find men to be far more annoying than men find women to be. I believe that this is primarily due to the remarkable differences in the brains of men and women. There are far more connections between neurons and neural sectors in a woman's brain than there are in a man's brain. In other words, women are made to be more aware of their surroundings—hence they can be more easily annoyed.

A man who does not understand this crucial difference often makes the "fairness" defense when his wife points out his annoying habits. He thinks it's unfair for his wife to be annoyed at his behavior when he is not as annoyed at her behavior. He feels that his wife should accept his behavior just as he accepts hers. But the fact remains: Annoying habits rob Love Bank accounts. If a man wants his wife to be in love with him, when she finds his behavior annoying, he should take her complaints seriously and change his habits.

A word of warning: Making a list of annoying habits can be very risky because you both might interpret each other's list as a sign that you're not right for each other. Besides, you've already learned that criticism can be very hurtful, and the list itself could seem to be a real Love Buster. But if you view a change in your habits as a mutual effort to care for each other, and make sure that you are not being disrespectful when you bring them to each other's attention (say, "This bothers me, I'd love it if you could do this...," instead of "You look stupid whenever you do this—stop it!"), you can chip away at these annoying habits one at a time until you become even more compatible than you are now.

Alternative Behavior

Can you think of a specific, alternative behavior
to replace the following
annoying habit?

Annoying Habit: Leaving dirty clothes on the floor after use.

Alternative Behavior: Hang up clothes or put them in a dirty-clothes hamper.

Thought Questions

1. It's not always easy to explain your partner's annoying habits and hear about your own annoying habits. You may feel that you and your partner should accept each other "as is"—not trying to change anything. But why is it important to be honest about and willing to change these "little things"?

2. What happens to you and your partner's Love Bank account each time an annoying habit is used?

Independent Behavior

Independent behavior is activities that are planned and executed without much thought of your partner's feelings as if your partner doesn't exist.

Have you ever planned activities without considering your partner's feelings? You may have even known that he or she would not have approved, but you went ahead and did it anyway? If you've ever done that, you've invited this sixth Love Buster into your relationship—independent behavior.

Whenever you plan to do something good for you but bad for your partner, it's independent behavior. And because it will withdraw love units whenever you do it, it's a Love Buster. If you want to stay in love, you cannot make decisions as if you are independent. Your partner does exist, and he or she will  feel the effects of almost everything you do—you are interdependent. If you practice independent behavior, you'll create an incompatible lifestyle that will eventually destroy your love. But if you practice interdependent behavior, making decisions that are mutually acceptable, you will build compatibility and sustain your love.

I hear married couples say things like, "If Sam loved me, he'd let our cats sleep with us at night." Or "If Ellen were not so self-centered, she'd encourage me to go bowling with my friends every Thursday." It's as if they think only one partner needs care. But what about Sam? Don't his feelings count? And what about Ellen? Does her husband care at all about how she feels while he's out bowling?

If a husband and wife care about each other, neither will want the other to suffer. So when making plans, they discuss alternatives with each other until they find one that makes both of them happy.

Since independent behavior is so tricky to identify and overcome, yet so very important to avoid, two chapters will be devoted entirely to that destructive habit and how to avoid it. The reason I focus special attention on independent behavior is that it creates such incompatibility in marriage that few couples can survive, so you never want it to get a foothold in your marriage.

Once married, just about every decision you make will determine your compatibility. Career choices, financial decisions, the way you raise your children, the friends you choose, your leisure activities, and a host of other lifestyle issues will be decided one by one. And those decisions will be made either independently of each other's interests or with each other's interests in mind. If you make your decisions independently, the lifestyle you build will make both of you very incompatible and unhappy. It will destroy your love for each other. But if your decisions are made interdependently, with benefit to both of you, that lifestyle you create will make both of you compatible and happy. It will help sustain your love.

Alternative Behavior

Can you think of a specific, alternative behavior
to replace the following
independent behavior?

Independent Behavior: Saying "yes" for your family to attend a party for an extended family member without asking your spouse about his/her feelings or family schedule.

Alternative Behavior: Tell the person, *Let me get back to you in 5 minutes* (or enough time to contact your spouse, and avoid saying that you need to check with your spouse because that would make your spouse the "bad guy" if the answer is "no"). Then text or call your spouse asking, *How would you feel about going to this party with family on this date/time? Or I'd love it if we could attend the family party. How would you feel about this?* If your spouse is not enthusiastic about doing the activity and you want to do it, ask to negotiate together to identify a mutually enthusiastic plan (chapter Seventeen will help you with this negotiation process).

Action Step: Time for Self-Evaluation. On a piece of paper, write down the Love Busters you think you do to your partner that may cause him or her unhappiness (Disrespectful Judgments, Selfish Demands, Angry Outbursts, Independent Behavior, Annoying Habits, Dishonesty). From those you identified, rank them in order of how you think they hurt your partner. Then briefly identify alternative habits from the chapters that you'd like to try that will develop your protection skills. Starting now, have a zero-tolerance policy for your own Love Busters.

Keeping Love Busters Out of Your Marriage

Why are we tempted to make these six mistakes of selfish demands, disrespectful judgments, angry outbursts, dishonesty, annoying habits, and independent behavior? None should make any sense at all to a couple who wants to be in love. When they've promised to care for each other, why would they want to hurt each other?

It's really not that difficult to understand. While all of these habits may make our partner feel bad, for one reason or another they tend to make us feel good. We do them because we like to do them. Love Busters give us comfort or pleasure, and we have a difficult time resisting them, even when we know we do them at our partner's expense.

Love Busters exist in all marriages at one time or another—none of us is thoughtful 100 percent of the time. But you can minimize them in your marriage by taking the right precautions. As soon as you find a Love Buster starting to take hold, do whatever it takes to overcome it.

The second gift of love, protection, will keep your love for each other secure. When you protect each other from Love Busters, you will grow in compatibility. If you fail to protect, by allowing Love Busters to gain a foothold and grow, you will grow apart and all the care in the world will not save your marriage.

If you and your spouse have trouble controlling Love Busters, I recommend that you read Dr. Harley's book, *Love Busters: Overcoming Habits That Destroy Romantic Love* (Harley, 1992, 2008, 2016), or seek professional help to ensure a zero tolerance for your own Love Busters.

Thought Questions

1. Did you know God "hates" these Love Busters too? Proverbs 6:16-19 says, "There are six things the Lord hates, seven that are an abomination to him: haughty eyes [proud, judgmental], a lying tongue, hands that shed innocent blood, a heart that devises wicked plans, feet that make haste to run to evil, a false witness who breathes out lies, and one who sows discord among brothers." God hates these behaviors because He loves people and Love Busters hurt those He loves.

2. You probably are familiar with one of the most popular verses about love in the Bible. It starts with "Love is patient..." (1 Corinthians 13:4-7). But have you ever taken a closer look at how that verse defines love? It says, "Love is patient and kind; love does not envy or boast; it is not arrogant or rude. It does not insist on its own way; it is not irritable or resentful; it does not rejoice at wrongdoing, but rejoices with the truth." Out of the eight characteristics associated with love, how many are positive (meaning "doing") behaviors? Three: patient, kind, rejoices with truth. How many are negative (meaning "not doing") behaviors? FIVE! And can you see Love Busters in this definition? One of the most popular definitions of love tells us to protect others from our own Love Busters and care for others. **Love = care + protection!** I call this **Caring Love.**

15

Identify and Eliminate Love Busters

Jon and Kathy celebrated their 10th anniversary, but they were living apart for much of that time. Jon accepted a sales job soon after they were married, which required him to be away from Kathy from Monday through Thursday each week. They both agreed it was a temporary sacrifice for their future happiness. But their "temporary" decision created a financial lifestyle they couldn't live without. And there were other unexpected results: One was that Kathy and Jon developed habits leading to independent lives.

With each independent decision, more and more thoughtless habits and plans were being made. To make matters worse, they started fighting about each other's thoughtlessness. Love units were regularly being withdrawn and they were not happy.

Jon and Kathy knew something needed to change or their family's future was in jeopardy. So they agreed to make lifestyle changes that would restore their love. It started with a plan to protect each other from their own thoughtless habits.

Wouldn't it be great if you never hurt each other? Or if when one of you hurt the other by mistake, you would immediately apologize and take steps to avoid doing it again? Protection in marriage is actually more important than the care we discussed in the first part of this book. Once you allow Love Busters to enter your relationship, your spouse's desire to meet your needs begins to evaporate.

When a person is in pain due to Love Busters, he or she usually doesn't want to meet needs or even have needs met. So Love Busters not only withdraw love units that were deposited when emotional needs were met, but they also prevent more love units from being deposited. You may have already experienced how difficult it is to meet each other's emotional needs when one of you has been offended by the other. That's why it's critically important that you eliminate Love Busters to keep your Love Bank balances high.

Love Busters don't usually enter a relationship with a full-scale invasion. They often begin with a seemingly harmless foothold. But from this inauspicious beginning, they grow to become ugly, destructive habits that can ruin your marriage. If you have already allowed Love Busters to gain a foothold, they probably have not yet developed to maturity. But if you don't get rid of them now, they may ruin any hope of a lifetime of love together.

I suggest that you follow a four-step plan to help you identify and eliminate any Love Busters that may have nosed their way into your relationship. If you find any Love Busters, this plan will help you eliminate them quickly so they don't grow to do serious damage.

Step 1: Identify Love Busters

Before you go to battle, you need to know your enemy. If you're battling Love Busters, you need to know what they are and how they express themselves. Earlier, I identified six broad types of Love Busters that can turn us all into monsters. Which of these are especially threatening to your relationship, and what specific behavior is involved?

One partner is often ignorant of the things he or she does to hurt the other. Love Busters can become second nature—habits we don't even know we have. Frequently the perpetrator doesn't even remember doing them. That's why the person on the receiving end of these Love Busters has to identify them because he or she is the one who feels the pain. You must tell each other what makes you unhappy.

To do this, review the six categories of Love Busters I described previously. Consider whether any are present in your relationship. For each Love Buster your partner exhibits, write down: 1) how often it occurs; 2) the form it takes (use an additional sheet of paper if needed); 3) the form it takes that hurts you the most; 4) when the behavior started; and 5) how it has developed.

Step 2: Identify Love Busters that Cause the Greatest Pain

In some marriages, all six types of Love Busters ruin the relationship. But for most, it's only two or three that cause most of the problems. Whether all six are present, or only two, each partner should begin by focusing most of their attention on the one that's the worst. Once there is a handle on it, then the next most troublesome Love Buster can be addressed.

To help your partner choose which Love Busters should be tackled first, rank the Love Busters in terms of their impact on your relationship. Decide which Love Buster causes you the greatest unhappiness and rank that number 1. Continue ranking the Love Busters on your list until you have ranked them all.

Step 3: Agree to Eliminate Love Busters for Each Other

It's easy for you to understand why your partner should change to protect you. It's usually more difficult to understand why you should change to protect him or her. However, if you are to give each other the gift of protection, it's essential that you believe each other's assertion that changes are necessary.

As a concrete act of protection, I suggest that you make a commitment to eliminate the Love Busters that your partner has identified. As mentioned before, to help you formalize your intentions, at the end of this book, you will have an opportunity to sign the Marital Promise that commits to overcoming Love Busters.

None of us likes to be criticized, and when we are, we often react defensively. So if you're not careful, you may respond to your partner's revelations with disrespect and anger—two of the very Love Busters you are trying to eliminate. If you react that way, disrespectful judgments and angry outbursts are Love Busters that may need your special attention.

When you read each other's list, be careful to accept the evaluation with the gift of protection in mind. Your lists will help you discover areas of weakness, and you may feel hurt by what you read. Remember, this is simply information that will help you do a better job protecting each other.

Step 4: Eliminate the Love Busters

You may not have had enough time for your bad habits to be deeply imprinted, so you should be able to eliminate them quickly. You may find that it's simply a matter of agreeing to do it. Once you've decided to do it, you may find that you never indulge in the bad habits again.

But for some habits, it isn't quite that simple. Deeply-rooted habits require a plan to follow and someone to hold you accountable to complete the plan. If you find that you continue to hurt your partner after you have made a reasonable effort to overcome the Love Busters, you may need professional help to overcome it. Marriage-support groups sponsored by churches and community organizations enable couples to overcome Love Busters by being accountable to others in the group. The group will check up on you, holding you to your promises.

Or you may want to ask a professional marriage counselor to hold you accountable. They are trained to teach you how to change your behavior, monitor your progress and remind you of your commitment. But if change doesn't take place quickly, find another marriage counselor to help you. Act quicky to overcome Love

Busters, because they do so much damage. If your relationship is to survive, you must stop them in their tracks.

To be certain the Love Busters do not invade your marriage, I encourage you to revisit this conversation each year, along with the emotional needs. It will help remind you to continue fulfilling your promise to protect. As a reminder, if you would like to read more on this subject, try my books, *Love Busters: Overcoming Habits That Destroy Romantic Love* (Harley, 1992, 2016) and its accompanying workbook, *Five Steps to Romantic Love* (Harley, 1993, 2002). In addition, to help remember your plan to eliminate Love Busters, you may want to download and use *The Gift of Protection* mobile app from FourGiftsofLove.org and Apple App Store.

Thought Questions

1. If your partner identified annoying habits, did that discourage you? Remember, you have the ability to change your habits. It might be uncomfortable at first, like folding your arm the opposite way, but with practice, these new habits can become as effortless as the old habits. And you'll avoid the automatic withdrawal of valuable love units.

2. Did you remember to thank your partner for giving honest feedback about your love-busting behaviors? Sometimes it's difficult to hear, but you definitely need honesty from your partner...if you want to keep your promise and succeed at giving your gifts of love.

16

The Policy of Joint Agreement, Part I

Love Busters will always stand in the way of your marital happiness. If you allow these habits to grow, you may become so dissatisfied with your marriage that it may not last very long. Selfish demands, disrespectful judgments, angry outbursts, dishonesty, annoying habits, and independent behavior—they are all dangerous habits that threaten every marriage.

Your gift of protection will help guard you against Love Busters. By agreeing not to be the source of each other's unhappiness, it will be much easier for you to identify destructive habits whenever they show their ugly faces. That's because you now know that whenever you're demanding, disrespectful, angry, annoying, dishonest, or engaged in independent behavior, you are hurting your partner— something you have promised to avoid.

With the goal of the total elimination of Love Busters, I've written a policy to help you protect each other in marriage. This policy will help you avoid all six Love Busters, but it is especially helpful in eliminating independent behavior, the primary cause of marital incompatibility. By following it, you will create a lifestyle that will protect both of you from each other's selfish and destructive tendencies. I call it The Policy of Joint Agreement: *Never do anything without an enthusiastic agreement between you and your spouse.* If you make all your decision together and avoid final choices until they are in your mutual interest, you build a partnership that will last for life.

The Policy of Joint Agreement: Never do anything without an enthusiastic agreement between you and your spouse.

The reason that the Policy of Joint Agreement protects you so well is that it forces you to 1) make mutually compatible decisions, and 2) take each other's feelings into account before you act or make decisions. This means that when you're tempted to make demands, show disrespect, lose your temper, lie, or persist in annoying habits, you're reminded to avoid doing any of those things. But the agreement is especially useful in helping you  avoid independent behavior because it gives your spouse a chance to veto thoughtless plans.

You may have already been following this policy without ever being told what it is. If so, that is why you feel so safe with each other. But there are times when both of you will be tempted to make decisions that are not acceptable to the other, and when you are tempted, the Policy of Joint Agreement should be there to prevent you from making a disastrous mistake of gaining at each other's expense.

Creating a Compatible Lifestyle

Building your life together is like building a house. Each brick is a choice you make about the way you live together. If you follow the Policy of Joint Agreement and make choices that are mutually agreeable, your house will be strong and beautiful. But if some bricks are acceptable to only one of you, those weak bricks will make your whole house an uncomfortable place to live.

Compatibility means that you live in harmony with each other. It means enjoying the lifestyle you created because it is what both of you want and need. Each brick that goes into your house has been chosen to make both of you comfortable.

Incompatibility, on the other hand, is created when the Policy of Joint Agreement is not followed—when one partner chooses bricks that are in his or her own best interest only. All acts of selfishness, that are at the other's expense not only withdraw love units but also undermine the very fabric of marriage—safety and trust. Incompatibility, therefore, is simply the result of accumulating thoughtless habits and activities. The more of them a couple accumulates, the more incompatible they become.

> Compatibility means that you live in harmony with each other. It means enjoying the lifestyle you created because it is what both of you want and need.

Most marriages begin with very little independent behavior because successful courting usually avoids it. Couples who are considering marriage make a special effort to behave thoughtfully because if they don't, they won't get to the altar.

But after marriage, independent behavior usually begins to appear. In the names of personal freedom, private interests, and expanding horizons, spouses develop habits and activities that do not take each other's feelings into account. Before long, they are no longer compatible.

An affair is an extreme but common example of what happens when a couple becomes incompatible. Spouses are unfaithful to each other because having an affair temporarily meets their emotional needs and makes them feel good. The fact that it hurts their spouse more than anything else they could do does not deter them. An affair creates instant incompatibility because as long as it's tolerated, there's no way that a couple can live together in harmony. It's a single brick that threatens to destroy the entire house.

You may be uncomfortable with my example because you assume that an affair could never happen to your marriage. But my own research and the research of others indicate that it happens in over 60 percent of marriages. It's the most common complaint I hear from couples I counsel. Think about it. If you can avoid an affair during your marriage, you will be in the minority!

Both unfaithful and betrayed spouses I've counseled never thought it would happen to them. Unfaithful spouses thought they had a strong enough character to resist temptation, and betrayed spouses felt that a good marriage required blind trust in each other. They didn't know that unless they took special precautions, they would fall prey to infidelity. And they didn't know that the Policy of Joint Agreement was the backbone of those precautions.

Infidelity usually comes not as an isolated failure to follow the Policy of Joint Agreement in these marriages; rather, it follows a host of decisions made by both spouses that failed to take each other's feelings into account. In fact, couples that fall victim to infidelity are usually in the habit of *not* taking each other's feelings into account. They build marriages in which they make independent decisions that create independent lifestyles that I call *secret second lives*. It's in these secret second lives that romantic relationships outside of marriage flourish.

The bottom line is that couples should eliminate behavior that is good for one and bad for the other. In the long run, the gains from having a mutually agreeable lifestyle more than outweigh the loss of an independent lifestyle. But thoughtless behavior is not easy to avoid. Most people feel resentful if they must give up something they enjoy, even if participating in it makes the one they love unhappy.

Resentment and Independent Behavior

How do you feel about avoiding independent behavior? If your partner were not enthusiastic about your plans for the weekend, and you were to abandon them to accommodate his or her feelings, would you feel resentful? At this point in your relationship, this may not be a problem because you would recognize your plan for what it is—thoughtless behavior. Neither of you may feel resentful about changing plans that turn out to be thoughtless. But I guarantee that there will be a point in your marriage when resentment will accompany your effort to follow the Policy of Joint Agreement. In an effort to anticipate this problem, we'll discuss it now.

There are two kinds of resentment: 1) resentment due to a partner's thoughtless behavior or activity (*action*); and 2) resentment due to not being able to do a thoughtless behavior or activity (*inaction*). In other words, the first would take place when your partner decides to do something that bothers you, while the second would occur when you avoid something you would like to do because it bothers your partner.

Resentment caused by a partner's thoughtless behavior or activity is a much greater problem in marriage than resentment caused by missing out on something. That's because thoughtlessness *always* leads to Love Bank withdrawals—there are no harmless alternatives. But if your partner doesn't enthusiastically agree with a decision you want to make, while you may be required to give up that one choice, there are countless other choices that would make both of you happy. A little creative thought and *poof*—your resentment

> There are two kinds of resentment: 1) resentment due to a partner's thoughtless behavior or activity (*action*); and 2) resentment due to not being able to do a thoughtless behavior or activity (*inaction*).

disappears when you find an alternative choice that satisfies both of you.

The first kind of resentment is much greater than the second—that's why the Policy of Joint Agreement has a "default key": Never do anything that causes your partner unhappiness even if it will cause you resentment that comes from inaction. But this is only a short-term solution to *avoid* being the cause of your partner's unhappiness—the problem isn't solved yet. The Policy of Joint Agreement still *forces* couples to negotiate until a *mutually* enthusiastic decision is finally reached.

The Policy of Joint Agreement's Default Key: Never do anything that causes your partner unhappiness even if it will cause you resentment that comes from inaction.

To illustrate, let's look at the life of Kathy and Jon. Kathy had an opportunity to attend an office party, but she knew that Jon would not want her to go without him. Since spouses were not invited and she wanted to go, she simply went to the party alone. She let him know about her plans by leaving a message on their answering machine.

Jon experienced the first kind of resentment. Kathy chose to do something that made her feel good but made her husband feel bad. She justified it as something she had to do for her job. Besides, she reasoned, marriage was not slavery and Jon had no right to try to control her behavior by telling her where she could and could not go.

What made Jon resentful was that Kathy did something that hurt him, and she didn't even care how he felt about it. When she finally arrived home at 4:00 a.m., he was still awake and was an emotional wreck. Kathy argued that he was upset because he had chosen to be upset, not because she had done anything wrong.

There was nothing Jon could say to convince Kathy that it was her thoughtless behavior that upset him. He concluded that she did not care about how he felt, and that made him even more resentful.

Jon had a great deal of trouble recovering from Kathy's night out because her thoughtlessness struck at the very core of their relationship. Her decision proved to him that his feelings were not important to her.

But what about Kathy's feelings? If Jon cared about Kathy, wouldn't he have sacrificed his own feelings (i.e., been willing to suffer) so that she could have a good time?

That brings up a dangerous practice: Sacrificing for each other. Suppose Kathy had asked Jon how he felt about her attending the party alone, and he had felt uncomfortable about her going alone. But instead of expressing his reservations, he would have told her that he wanted her to go so that she could enjoy herself. Wouldn't his sacrifice, or suffering for her benefit, have been a sign of love? Isn't that what caring spouses should do for each other—sacrifice their own interests so that their spouse can enjoy life? Not if their care is mutual.

If Kathy and Jon care for each other, neither should want the other to suffer. Kathy's decision to go to the party, knowing that Jon would be unhappy, is thoughtless. Even if he were willing to suffer so she could enjoy the evening, her care for him should not let him suffer. If they both care for each other, the only decision that would reflect mutual care is the one that makes them both happy.

Let's imagine a different scenario for this couple. Suppose Kathy had asked Jon *how he would feel if* she went to the office party, and Jon told her that he *wasn't enthusiastic* about the idea. If Kathy had decided not to go to the party, she would have been vulnerable to the second kind of resentment; she could have been resentful for having to *give up* a good time just because Jon didn't approve. She could have thought, *He doesn't care enough about me to want me to have fun.*

But she would not experience the second kind of resentment if they were to discover an alternative that they could both enthusiastically accept. And that's precisely what couples that follow the Policy of Joint Agreement learn how to do—find mutually acceptable alternatives. Through respectful negotiation, Kathy and Jon would immediately search for a solution to the problem that would satisfy both of them. And when that solution was found, it would eliminate any resentment.

Thought Questions

1. If you and your partner have identified Love Busters in your relationship, you may be tempted to think that you're not right for each other. What happens if you practice new habits to replace those bad habits, will you become more compatible?

2. If you guard each other from your Love Busters throughout your lives together, could you keep growing in compatibility? Why?

3. Why is the Policy of Joint Agreement essential in building a compatible lifestyle? (Hint: What does it *force* you both to do?)

17

The Policy of Joint Agreement, Part II

Whenever you and your partner have a conflict of interests and cannot agree on a decision, there is a procedure that I recommend. It will help you get into the habit of making mutually acceptable decisions by following the Policy of Joint Agreement.

How to Negotiate with the Policy of Joint Agreement

The more you practice this procedure, the quicker you'll be able to come to an enthusiastic agreement about almost any issue that comes your way.

1. Set ground rules to make negotiations pleasant and safe. Before you start to negotiate, agree with each other that you will both follow these rules: 1) be pleasant and cheerful throughout your discussion of the issue; 2) put safety first—do not make demands, show disrespect, or become angry when you negotiate, even if your negotiations fail; and 3) if you reach an impasse, stop for a while and come back to the issue later. Your negotiations should respect your differences in feelings and perspectives. Otherwise, you will fail to make them pleasant and safe.

Suggestion: If you can't come to the negotiation table with the ability to make a smile, then pick another time when you are in a better mood. If you can't smile, you aren't in control of your emotions. It is essential to make negotiation pleasant—otherwise, you won't accomplish anything.

2. *Identify the problem from the perspectives of both you and your partner.* Be able to state each other's position on the issue before you go on to find a solution. Each of you should describe what you would like and why you would like it. Then explain the other's position to each other's satisfaction. Be sure you fully understand each other before you go any further toward an agreement. And respect your differences of opinion. To illustrate, I will again use the example of Kathy and Jon.

Spouses were not invited to Kathy's office party. Many companies like Kathy's think that such a policy helps build morale at work, but it usually does the opposite: It creates serious problems for families and businesses. Instead of integrating families into the business, it sends a strong message that its policy is to compete with families for the time and attention of a spouse. Such a policy forces a husband or wife to choose between the business and the family.

If Kathy had been in the habit of negotiating with the Policy of Joint Agreement, as soon as she knew about the party, she would have told Jon about it and let him know that she wanted to attend. Then, she would have asked the crucial question: *How do you feel about it?*

Jon would have responded by expressing his concerns without being critical of Kathy's wish to go to the party, by first saying, *I'm not enthusiastic about you going to the party alone* (or using a 1-5 rating scale). *Could we negotiate this together?* Then he could share emotional honesty by explaining his fear of her being vulnerable to some men at work meeting her emotional needs. He could also explain that he didn't like being left home alone while she was out having a good time. But he would have made a disrespectful judgment if he had expressed shock that she would even think of doing such a thing without him.

Again, if Kathy were to tell Jon that his reasons were stupid, that would also have been a disrespectful judgment. It probably would have led to a fight. So to respect his reasons for feeling the way he did, she should try to accommodate them in a final resolution of the conflict.

Suggestion: Try to keep your perspectives brief (around 3-4 sentences each). This ensures that you focus only on what you want and why, avoiding disrespectful judgments and demands. After each perspective is stated, have the listening spouse restate exactly what he or she heard. By keeping the perspectives short and to the point, each spouse can more accurately restate what was heard.

3. *Brainstorm solutions with abandon.* Spend some time thinking of ways to handle the problem. Let it incubate so that your brain can work on it for a while. There are thousands of possibilities that your brain will sort through, discarding those that are flawed and holding on to those that might work. Carry a pad of paper or cell phone to record those possible solutions that come to mind. And don't correct each other when you hear of a plan that you don't like—you'll have a chance to do that when you come to the fourth step.

By negotiating with each other before making a decision about the office party, Jon and Kathy would have tried to find a way to achieve her goal with his objections in mind. If Kathy were to go to the party without Jon, he would be offended. If she were to stay at home with Jon, she would be frustrated. What could they do that would make both of them happy? All possible solutions would have to address the opinions and feelings of Jon and Kathy. By addressing the issue as soon as Kathy knew about it, they had time to let their brains go to work on the problem.

Suggestion: Get out a piece of paper and write down possible solutions to the problem that you might both agree to enthusiastically. Try to think "outside of the box." And remember: Don't evaluate any option at this time.

4. *Choose the solution that is appealing to both of you that best meets the conditions of the* Policy of Joint Agreement—*mutual and enthusiastic agreement.* From your list of possible solutions, some will satisfy only one of you but not both. However, scattered within the list will be solutions that both of you find attractive. Among those solutions that are mutually satisfactory, select the one that you both like the most. But if you can't find one that you both agree to enthusiastically, go back to step 3 and continue to brainstorm.

One possible solution that might appeal to both Kathy and Jon would begin with Kathy asking her co-workers if they felt concerned about the no-spouse rule. If there were others who thought that spouses should be invited, they could all meet with the manager to try to change the rule.

In this particular case that I witnessed, that's what Jon proposed to Kathy, and she liked the idea. When she met with her coworkers, she was surprised to discover that most of them wanted their spouses to attend the party. At a meeting with the office manager, Kathy and others in the office were able to convince the manager that family-friendly policies were good business. Not only did Jon and Kathy attend the office party together that year, but the change in office policy also meant that they would be attending all of the office parties together from that day forward.

Suggestion: On the left-side margin of the brainstorm paper, put your initials at the top with a vertical line down where you can both write down your vote for each option using a 1-5 rating scale, with 5 being very enthusiastic and 1 being very unenthusiastic. The votes with mutual 4s and/or 5s would have the greatest potential for success. But if there is a 3 and a 4 rating, then go to the one who rated the choice a 3 and ask, "How would you change this option so that it would be a 4 for you?" Write down the option or come up with some variations, and both vote again. Keep negotiating until you both have at least a 4 for an option.

That's what the Policy of Joint Agreement can do for your lifestyle. It doesn't change just one event; it sets a precedent for future events. Each time you find a solution that meets the conditions of the Policy of Joint Agreement you add another strong brick to your house.

At first, this four-step procedure may seem formal, awkward, and time-consuming. Listing possible solutions sounds like it could take weeks to solve simple problems. But once you get the hang of it, your improved skills will be up to speed. Eventually, you go through those steps so quickly and effortlessly that you can do them almost anywhere and anytime.

Remember, every time you try to force your partner into a way of life that is unpleasant, you are chipping away at his or her love for you. Not only is it a thoughtless way to accomplish your objectives, but it also won't get the job done. Sooner or later your partner will escape you and your unpleasant way of life. You can build a far more enjoyable lifestyle for yourself by taking your partner's feelings into account. It's not only the thoughtful thing to do, but it will also build your love for each other.

The Policy of Joint Agreement will help your decisions stand up to the test of time. They will be decisions that will provide a strong foundation for your life together. With it, neither of you will be a slave or a master, and you won't feel alone or abandoned in your effort to achieve your important objectives. You will become each other's willing partner in building a life of love and care.

Create a Compatible Lifestyle with the Promise of Protection

Your lifestyle is the accumulation of all your habits and activities that make up the life you live. Before marriage, each of you created your own individual lifestyle that made you happy: You chose your job, your car, your residence, and even each other because it's what each of you wanted individually.

But your lifestyle changes as soon as you marry. Every day you are making decisions that will form a new lifestyle—your married lifestyle. With each decision, new habits and activities will begin to take shape. They will form the framework for a structure that will be in the process of completion for years to come. If you are not careful, though, you may create a lifestyle that may work for one of you and drive the other crazy.

Now is the time to realize that your married lifestyle must be created with mutual consideration. The lifestyle you choose must be carefully selected to make *both* of you very happy. That's why the gift of protection must guide its creation. With this special gift, you will protect each other from your self-centeredness whenever you make a decision.

> The lifestyle you choose must be carefully selected to make *both* of you very happy.

Does Complaining Violate the Gift of Protection

The lifestyle you and your spouse create in marriage will require many adjustments. A plan that both of you once thought would be great may turn out to be not so great, at least for one of you. When that happens, complaining usually begins.

If a complaint is made in a respectful way, it can be much-needed feedback that your lifestyle needs further adjustment. You may hear a complaint regarding an emotional need that is not being met or about a Love Buster that has crept into your life. Whatever the complaint is, it reflects the need for a change that will accommodate the spouse who's complaining.

But complaining can be a real showstopper if it's accompanied by demands, disrespect, or anger. If you want to withdraw love units in a hurry, try complaining with those three Love Busters.

Complaining itself isn't a Love Buster, but when it's made with demands, disrespect, or anger, your innocent request for change will lose its meaning. If your complaint simply takes the form of a request for change, even though your partner may feel uncomfortable knowing that there's work ahead, it's not a Love Buster; it's honesty.

A complaint should lead to a plan of action that will solve the problem. If it's not possible to create a plan when the complaint is first made, schedule a time when you will be able to think it through carefully and agree to a solution. Remember, most of your complaints will involve habits, and a change of habit requires repetition. Your plan should include a description of the new habit or activity you desire and a way to provide practice until it becomes an effortless part of your lifestyle.

If you and your partner go into your marriage with a willingness to deal with complaints as soon as possible, respectfully and pleasantly, they will never overwhelm you. It's only when you let them pile up from years of neglect that you finally feel overwhelmed.

I have shown you how to negotiate with the Policy of Joint Agreement. If you learn to handle all of your complaints with this procedure, you will find yourselves eliminating your problems just about as fast as they arrive. And you will do it with protection, without hurting each other.

If you would like more specific help in learning how to create a compatible lifestyle, I recommend that you read *He Wins, She Wins: Learning the Art of Marital Negotiation* (Harley, 2013), and *Fall in Love, Stay in Love* (Harley, 2001). In addition, you may want to download and use the *Let's Negotiate* mobile app from FourGiftsofLove.org, Google Play, and Apple App Store.

⚙ *Talk About This*

Please remember to keep the conversation **BRIEF** and **STAY ON** the topic of the questions. And most importantly, use this time to practice your gifts of care and protection, being especially careful to avoid disrespectful comments. Remember, your goals are to be a source of happiness and avoid being a source of pain in your relationship.

1. Have you and your partner used these negotiation guidelines or something similar in the past or is this a new concept? Do you see how using these guidelines could help ensure your thoughtfulness to each other?

2. Are there problems that exist that require negotiation with your partner? Are you ready to get a negotiation workbook started and get on the path to a life of compatibility?

   Many couples have conflicts in their marriage that involve finances or budgeting, extended family, religion, career, and discipline of children. Conflicts in these categories usually take more time to resolve than a conflict over what one wears to a Bible study. So, schedule plenty of time to think about possible solutions and gather information; and get help going through the negotiation process, if needed for any "hot topic" conflicts.

   All conflicts can be resolved by using the Policy of Joint Agreement in negotiation. And when they are resolved this way, the Love Banks of each spouse are protected and a compatible lifestyle is created.

3. What are the four guidelines for successful negotiation? If you have your negotiation notebook, write a summary of these four guidelines on the back of the cover or first page.

4. Review the Negotiation Tips:

- Dedicate a spiral notebook for negotiation topics, identifying each conflict issue on its own page. (My recommendation is to buy a notebook with puppies or hearts or smiley faces...something to associate negotiation with a smile.)
- On the inside cover, list the four guidelines for negotiation, maybe abbreviated, along with any "suggestions" you want to remember (e.g., *Can I smile;* restating the other's perspective before stating your own; no comments-good or bad- after each brainstorm option).
- Schedule an agreed amount of time, like 30 minutes, each week to go through the negotiation process, one issue at a time. Often couples sweep the problem areas "under the rug," but the problems are still there. This alternative way is a plan and commitment to address the conflicts over time.
- If you have run out of brainstorm ideas and still have not come to a mutually enthusiastic solution, identify a mutually trusted friend or community leader (e.g., pastor), and ask for help with brainstorming ideas.
- One caution: I don't recommend spending more than 45 minutes per meeting. You will need your best thinking skills and emotional control during this time; going beyond 30-45 minutes will weaken those skills and control.

Supporting Research: A six-year, longitudinal study following 130 newlywed couples by John Gottman and colleagues identified several factors that led to long-term marital stability. Interestingly, a common technique used in marital therapy to promote communication skills, the active listening model, was "not predictive of differential marital outcomes" (Gottman, 1998, p. 17).

However, the predictive factors of divorce as indicated by the rigorous, longitudinal study were: 1) a husband's refusal to accept his wife's influence in making decisions; 2) the absence of the husband's ability to deescalate low-intensity negative situations; and 3) a wife's harsh start-up of conflict and negativity reciprocity in low-intensity negative situations.

A couple was happier and more stable if: 1) the husband accepted the wife's influence in decision making; 2) the husband was able to de-escalate a negative affect situation by being gentle and soothing; and 3) the wife had a softened "start-up" of conflict situations. Gottman concludes with a main observation: "Our data suggest that only newlywed men who accept influence from their wives are winding up in happy and stable marriages."

After reading the material in this book, Gottman's study seems to especially support the goals of the Policy of Joint Agreement and avoiding Love Busters in marriage. Would you agree?

(Gottman, J., Coan, J., Carrere, S., & Swanson, C. (1998). Predicting marital happiness and stability from newlywed interactions. *Journal of Marriage and Family, 60,* 5-22)

18

Why Are the Differences Between a Man and a Woman So Valuable in Marriage

arriage is between two entirely different kinds of people—a man and a woman—who complement each other in extraordinary ways. When they treat each other as equals, they both greatly benefit from their differences. By respecting each other's vastly different perspectives, and building their lives on the wisdom of those different perspectives, they grow together much wiser and stronger than either would ever be by themselves. But when each spouse ignores the other's perspective, making choices that benefit him or her independently, they lose that advantage which leads to unhappiness in marriage.

The position I've taken over the past 40 years that a man and woman are entirely different from each other has been very controversial. When I first wrote *His Needs, Her Needs* in 1986, many considered me to be far behind the times. But my background in neurophysiology convinced me of its truth very early. When I taught the course, physiological psychology, I was able to provide each student with a human brain to dissect, and there were both male and female brains distributed throughout the class. I wanted each student to notice the vast differences between them. They not only looked different, but they functioned differently. I wanted each student to fully understand why men and women think differently. It's because their brains are different.

Women have far more connections between the left and right hemispheres. The connecting band of fibers called the corpus callosum is much thicker in women than in men. There are more connections between neurons as well, and there are more neurons—about 12 billion more. And yet, their brain is smaller. I could go on and on describing the differences—how their brains develop differently, how they age differently, how their emotional expressions are triggered differently, how their abilities are reflected in differences, and, of course, how these differences are responsible for creating different emotional needs. There is a far greater difference between the brains of the average man and woman than there is between the brains of representative people of all racial groupings on earth. Racially and ethnically, we are essentially identical. Sexually, we are vastly different.

> Together they offer a more complete perspective on life than either can have on their own.

But while I demonstrated the differences between the brains of men and women to my students, I stressed their equal value. They complement each other. The strengths and weaknesses of male cognition balance the strengths and weaknesses of female cognition. Together they offer a more complete perspective on life than either can have on their own. All that's required for those specialized advantages to express themselves in real life was for every husband and wife to have profound respect for the differences in the way they viewed the world and think together to find mutually appealing solutions to the problems they face.

Throughout human history, however, their physical and mental differences have led to widespread discrimination by men against women. Sadly, we should not be surprised at that tragic result because whenever there have been differences among us, we have tended to discriminate. And since there are no greater differences than there are between a man and a woman, we should expect sexual discrimination. It's been just a little over 100 years that women have even had the right to vote in America because they were judged to be intellectually inferior. Instead of seeing women as an essential complement to their lives, men have tended to view them as personal property that were to serve them throughout life, much like slaves. Men viewed themselves as superior in every way and felt that the judgment of women was inadequate to make final decisions, even when it came to voting.

> Mutual respect in marriage means that the feelings and interests of both spouses are of value.

Thankfully, we have seen justice for women. Education, the ultimate equalizer, has proven that women are every bit as intelligent and creative as men. In fact, they are now the majority in most colleges and universities. Every male college student can attest to the fact that women are in no way intellectually inferior.

But while a man and woman are of equal value, they are not the same. A woman is a valuable complement to a man and a man is a valuable complement to a woman. Throughout my career, I've seen that difference benefit a husband and wife in marriage. I've witnessed how they need each other to become whole. And the wisdom that each one brings to a marital relationship raises each of them to a higher intellectual and moral level than they could have ever achieved on their own. But for that to happen, they must first and foremost respect and value each other.

I use the analogy of a husband and wife standing back-to-back, describing what they see to each other. Each is unable to see more than half of the horizon, but together they see it in its entirety. It would be a terrible mistake for either of them to claim that they had the only true vision of the world and that the other should be guided exclusively by their vision. It's only when they respect the differences in their perspectives and they learn from them, that they gain a complete knowledge of the world.

My primary reason for encouraging couples to value each other's opinions, perspectives, and interests is that their differences can help both of them create a greater life than either could have created on their own. Mutual respect in marriage means that the  feelings and interests of both spouses are of value. One spouse's interests should not dominate the interests of the other spouse. It's marital democracy. In this company called marriage, the spouses are co-CEOs.

But that doesn't mean that each spouse must lose their right to make decisions for personal benefit. It's just that their choice must also benefit the other spouse.

I'll illustrate that point with my cardinal rule of marriage, the Policy of Joint Agreement: *Never do anything without an enthusiastic agreement between you and your spouse.*

That rule focuses on mutual respect and consideration in marriage. Differences in physical strength, earning power, and even intelligence do not alter the equation. Power is granted to both spouses equally. But the default condition, doing nothing, would be a disaster if that became the norm. For a marriage to succeed, an agreement must be found, and that's where personal choice comes into the equation. It's assumed that both spouses are able to express their perspectives to each other and negotiate an outcome that works to the advantage of both. They are at liberty to do whatever works for both of them. Doing nothing ruins both of their lives.

When you decide to follow the Policy of Joint Agreement, you are giving each other equal power in your marriage. Neither of you can force the other to do anything or to put up with anything either of you decides to do. Your choices must work for both of you or you don't make them. With enthusiastic agreement as your goal with every conflict, you will learn to appreciate the differences in perspective that you bring to the issue. You will try to gain a better understanding of the vast differences in the way you both think and reason. It's only then that you'll be able to see what works best for each other, instead of trying to force your own way of thinking on each other.

> Marital problem-solving requires mutual respect, empathy, and understanding.

That's why marital problem-solving requires mutual respect, empathy, and understanding. Trying to demand compliance, or showing disrespect for your spouse's alternative point of view, or deciding to go it alone, making an independent choice, leads to marital failure. But it does more than that. It prevents you from coming to know an entirely different kind of person, someone not at all like you. It's someone who can make your understanding of the world much more complete if you regard that person as an equal, and show your profound respect for what he or she has to offer you in wisdom and support.

Thought Questions

1. Empathy is the ability to feel what someone else feels. If you both had empathy for each other, why would the gift of protection be easy to give? Why is this gift difficult to give when you don't have empathy for each other? What can you do to improve your ability to empathize?

2. Think about a few empathetic thoughts; thoughts that make you feel more understanding of your partner (e.g., *When s/he is upset, maybe there is something going on that I don't know about yet; Maybe s/he is seeing this problem from a perspective I don't understand yet.*

3. If a couple were empathetic, it would be as if they were wired together, feeling what each other feels. Although you are not directly wired into your partner, what's the next best thing you can do to understand how each of you thinks and feels? (Hint: "How do you think/feel about _____?")

19

Oneness

*O*uch! *That really hurt*, Sue cries out after Mark steps on her bare foot with his work boots. Mark immediately lifts his foot and also cries out in pain. *Ouch, that does hurt! I'm so sorry. I'll be more careful from now on.*

Does this scenario make sense? Do you wonder what planet they're from? Mark's foot is safely in his boot. Why would he feel her pain when he steps on her bare foot?

His reaction isn't consistent with our reality because we don't feel what others feel—we have to imagine the pain of others when we do something thoughtless. But if we did actually feel their pain, we would certainly be more thoughtful—to protect ourselves!

Because we can't actually feel what others feel, as married couples, we need a rule to compensate for our limited power of empathy. The Policy of Joint Agreement is that rule because it guarantees our mutual protection. A commitment to this policy will help you both avoid hurting each other in your marriage—making decisions to protect each other from your "work boots" as if you and your spouse are one.

Living as One with Your Spouse

An important characteristic of the gift of protection is a sense of interconnection—*your feelings become my feelings; your interests are my interests.*

In Mark 10:7-8 (NIV) we read, "'For this reason a man will leave his father and mother and be united to his wife, and the two will

become one flesh.' So they are no longer two, but one." And in 1 Corinthians 7:4 we read, "The wife gives authority over her body to her husband, and the husband gives authority over his body to his wife."

God's word is telling us that a husband and wife should think of themselves as interconnected—everything you do will not only affect yourself, but also your spouse. Sound familiar?

In marriage we are not independent or dependent—we're interdependent! And our decisions and behaviors need to reflect this important fact. In Ephesians 5:28-29 we read, "In the same way, husbands should love their wives as their own bodies. He who loves his wife loves himself. For no one ever hated his own flesh, but nourishes and cherishes it...." Once we marry, we identify ourselves with our spouse—two become one.

> Once we marry, we identify ourselves with our spouse— two become one.

Living as One with God, Through Christ

Similarly, once we become Christians, we identify ourselves with Christ. We are no longer our own but interconnected with God— living as one, through Christ. And 1 Corinthians 6:17, 19 reminds us of this by saying, "But he who is joined to the Lord becomes one spirit with him...Or do you not know that your body is a temple of the Holy Spirit within you, whom you have from God? You are not your own."

It's very clear in Scripture that God commands us to avoid our thoughtless behavior towards one another because He is affected by our actions (Ephesians 4:30-32). So if we care about pleasing

God and want to avoid causing Him grief, we will care about the feelings of others.

Unfortunately, when we become a Christian or when we become married, we don't go through a "oneness" machine—our feelings aren't automatically interconnected and we don't suddenly become thoughtful. And even when our rational mind tells us to avoid thoughtlessness, our instincts and habits can encourage us to make thoughtless decisions at times.

That's why we need to follow the Policy of Joint Agreement in marriage as a way to help compensate for our thoughtless instincts and habits. But I'd like to take this policy one step further— consider a version that reminds us that we are also one with God.

Mutual Enthusiastic Agreement Between God, Your Spouse, and You

You've probably heard the metaphor that describes a strong marriage as a rope with three strands where God is the third strand, strengthening the relationship between a husband and wife. But it's important to recognize that God's "strand" is not like the other two—it's the strongest. When you include God's wisdom in your daily decisions, your choices will be the best!

As a reminder of this fact, many Christians wear a bracelet that's inscribed, "WWJD" (What Would Jesus Do?). It's a memory trigger to seek God's wisdom and guidance in their moment-by-moment decisions—big or small.

The Policy of Joint Agreement is a reminder to include your spouse's wisdom in every decision you make. But why limit it to your spouse? Why not also include God's wisdom in every decision by asking, "Would He AND my spouse be enthusiastic about the choice I'm about to make?"

So I suggest a revision of this rule that includes God's interests and will for your life: Never do anything without an enthusiastic agreement between God, your spouse, and you. When you follow the Christian's version of the Policy of Joint Agreement, you will be giving your spouse and God your gift of protection.

> A Christian's version of the POLICY OF JOINT AGREEMENT: Never do anything without an enthusiastic agreement between God, your spouse, and you.

If you want to be more in tune with each other and God, I recommend our couple's devotional book, *Draw Close* (Harley/Harley, 2011).

Thought Questions

1. Why is it difficult to remember that God and your spouse are affected by your actions? What question could you ask God or your spouse that would help you follow the Policy of Joint Agreement?

2. James 2:18b says, "Show me your faith apart from your works, and I will show you my faith by my works." No one perfectly shows faith through their behaviors, but our faith motivates us to create plans to improve. If you habitually create a lifestyle of pain and suffering for your spouse, what are your works saying about your faith? As Christians, our inner motivation to protect our spouse (and others) comes from our faith and a desire to express our faith.

3. So, what is your inner motivation for protecting your spouse? What is your motivation to implement a specific plan to eliminate every Love Buster (having a no-tolerance policy for your own Love Busters)? Suggestion: Write down your motivation on a sticky note as a reminder of why you are creating thoughtful habits of protection and review this daily.

PART THREE

The Gift of Honesty

I PROMISE TO BE
COMPLETELY HONEST
WITH YOU

20

The Gift of Honesty with God

I am amazed when I think about God wanting me as His child—a single person out of billions on this earth and across thousands of years. "See what great love the Father has lavished on us, that we should be called children of God! And that is what we are!" (1 John 3:1 NIV) But even more amazing is the fact that He wants a deep and complete relationship—an open and honest relationship. He wants nothing hidden, nothing private, and nothing secret.

God's Gift of Honesty

God gives us His gift of honesty through His written word and His Spirit—working together to help us know Him more completely.

The Bible is the most remarkable book ever written. There is no other book that provides such complete information about God. It's no wonder that more Bibles have been printed and that there are more translations of the Bible than any other book in history. God spoke through over forty different writers from various walks of life and various times in history to present a cohesive and internally consistent revelation of who He is and what He wants from us.

But what's more remarkable is that through the gift of the Holy Spirit, we gain an even greater understanding of God. In 1 Corinthians 2:9-12, 16, we read that God's Spirit has revealed to us the "mind of Christ." And although our limited minds cannot comprehend *everything* about Him, through His Spirit we can have a better understanding of how He thinks and who He is.

Our Gift of Honesty to God

Through the Bible and the Holy Spirit, God has given us His gift of honesty. But have you considered what it takes to be honest with God? You might be wondering why we need to be honest with Him in the first place—after all, He already knows everything. Jesus confirmed this when He told His disciples "...for your Father knows what you need before you ask him" (Matthew 6:8). But then Jesus went on to give them a template for prayer (vv. 9-13). And Jesus, Himself, spent hours in communication with God. In 1 Thessalonians 5:17 we read, "pray without ceasing...for this is the will of God in Jesus Christ for you."

God wants us to be honest about our *understanding of Him* and *ourselves*. "But who do you say that I am?" Jesus asked Peter (Mark 8:29). "You are the Christ," the anointed One of God, was Peter's honest response. Unfortunately, our responses aren't always honest. Romans 1 reminds us that all humanity tends to exchange the truth about God for a lie. While His Holy Spirit reveals to us accurate information about who God really is, when we are tempted to sin, we tend to mask the truth with a lie saying, "God isn't who He is and isn't the One deserving our obedience, honor, and respect." Or, we claim that God has changed His mind about sin saying, "Now God accepts sinful behavior."

Why do we become liars? Because we don't want to face who we are. And who are we? We're sinners who don't deserve the fellowship and grace that He offers us. Honesty means we come before Him in humility, being truthful about who we are and who God is.

God wants a two-way, loving relationship: We take the time to receive His gift of honesty—learning about Him through the Bible and allowing His Spirit to reveal God's Truth; and we take the time to give Him this gift—telling Him our every thought and every plan because we want an honest relationship with Him.

Action Step: Take a few minutes right now to let God know that you want an honest relationship with Him. If you aren't used to honestly talking to God about who He is and who you are, here's a structure to help you get started:

1. Give praises to God.
2. Confess the sinful behavior you have done that day and commit to a plan for change.
3. Give thanks.
4. Tell Him your concerns and ask for what you desire.

Thought Questions

1. In what ways are you honest with God?

2. As a marriage counselor who specializes in infidelity, I've noticed that many Christians try to avoid God when they are involved in an affair. Like Adam and Eve, they try to hide their disobedience from Him by avoiding church, Bible study, and prayer. Why is it so difficult to give God the gift of honesty when you are not giving Him the gift of protection?

21

What Is Honesty

The subject of honesty in marriage was previously introduced to you with the first gift, care—being each other's primary source of happiness by meeting each other's most important emotional needs. If you or your partner selected honesty and openness as an emotional need that should be met in your marriage, you will be honest as one of the ways you care for each other.

Then honesty was addressed again when you learned about the second promise, protection—your promise to avoid being the source of each other's unhappiness by avoiding Love Busters. One of the six Love Busters that causes unhappiness in marriage is dishonesty. If you are to protect each other from your destructive and selfish predispositions, you will be honest with each other.

Since we have already discussed this topic of honesty twice, you may wonder why I bring it up again. Doesn't it seem like overkill to make it the third gift? Not really.

I've raised honesty to the level of a specific gift because it has a unique purpose in marriage. Honesty is more than an emotional need that must be met to sustain love and more than a way to avoid unhappiness. Honesty is absolutely essential if you and your spouse will ever come to understand each other. Without honesty, you will never make adjustments crucial to the creation of compatibility in your marriage. Without honesty, your best efforts to resolve conflicts will be wasted because you will not know each other well enough to find mutually acceptable solutions.

Honesty Helps You Aim at the Right Target

Most couples do their best to make each other happy—at least in the beginning of their marriage. But their efforts, however sincere, are often misdirected. They aim at the wrong target.

Imagine a man who buys his wife flowers every night on the way home from work. What a thoughtful thing to do—except his wife is allergic to them. Because she appreciates the gesture, she never mentions her allergies but just sniffles in silence. Soon, however, she begins to dread the thought of her husband coming home with those terrible flowers. Meanwhile, he's getting bored with the marriage because she is always feeling lousy and never has energy to do anything—because of her allergies. But of course, he won't tell her that.

Their marriage is in trouble not because of a lack of effort but because of their ignorance—ignorance caused by a lack of honesty. He thinks he's making her happy by bringing home flowers, but he doesn't realize that it's the cause of both their malaise. Let's say that, in his effort to show even more love for her, he brings home more and more flowers. Ultimately, she collapses on the couch, gasping for breath, surrounded by flowers, while he wonders why she doesn't seem to appreciate his kindness.

It's a preposterous story, but it portrays the way many couples miss the mark in their attempts to please each other. Their lack of honesty keeps them from correcting their real problems. Husbands and wives often misinform each other about their feelings, activities, and plans. This not only leads to Love Bank withdrawals when the deception is discovered, but it also makes marital conflicts impossible to resolve. As conflicts pile up, the dishonest couple is tempted to draw the conclusion that they're simply incompatible. They fail to understand that it's their dishonesty that's the culprit. They would grow in compatibility if only they would be honest with each other.

You may agree with me that spouses should be honest, but you may wonder how far honesty should go. You may feel that there are exceptions where honesty would create more trouble than it's worth. So to help you understand that this gift is for total honesty, not partial honesty, I have written a policy to guide you. I call it the *Policy of Radical Honesty*. I give it that name because total honesty is considered radical in a culture where dishonesty seems to reign.

The Policy of Radical Honesty: Reveal to your partner as much information about yourself as you know; your thoughts, feelings, habits, likes and dislikes, personal history, daily activities, and plans for the future.

To make this policy easier to understand, I've broken it down into five parts:

1. *Emotional Honesty*: Reveal your emotional reactions—both positive and negative—to the events of your life, particularly to your partner's behavior.

2. *Historical Honesty*: Reveal information about your personal history, particularly events that demonstrate personal weakness or failure.

3. *Current Honesty*: Reveal information about events of your day. Provide your partner with a calendar of your activities, with special emphasis on those that may affect him or her.

4. *Future Honesty*: Reveal your thoughts and plans regarding future activities and objectives.

5. *Complete Honesty*: Do not leave your partner with a false impression about your thoughts, feelings, habits, likes and

dislikes, personal history, daily activities, or plans for the future. Do not deliberately keep personal information from your partner.

To some extent, this rule seems like motherhood and apple pie. Who would argue that it's *not* a good idea to be honest? But in my years of experience as a marriage counselor, I have found that many clients consider dishonesty to be a good idea under certain conditions.

To those who argue that dishonesty can be justified occasionally, I must say that the Policy of Radical Honesty leaves no room for exceptions. And because there are so many who *advocate* dishonesty in marriage, I need to build a case for my position. Let's take a careful look at each of the five parts of this policy.

Emotional Honesty

Some people find it difficult to express their emotional reactions, particularly the negative ones. They may fear that others will judge them for their feelings or they may tell themselves they should not feel the way they do. They may doubt their ability to express negative feelings without demands, disrespect, or anger. Or they may think they should be unconditionally accepting and complaints should never be uttered.

> **Emotional Honesty:** Reveal your emotional reactions—both positive and negative—to the events
> of your life, particularly to your partner's behavior.

But negative feelings serve a valuable purpose in marriage: They are a signal that something is wrong. If you successfully steer clear of selfish demands, disrespectful judgments, and angry outbursts, your expression of negative feelings can help you and your partner make your marriage much more enjoyable.

Honesty is the first step in making appropriate adjustments to each other. And a good marriage requires continual adjustments. Both of you will grow and change throughout life and if you want to grow together, you should adjust to each other's changes. But how can you know how to adjust if you're not receiving accurate information? That's flying blind, like a pilot at night without an instrument panel.

Of course, the mere communication of negative reactions does not assure an adjustment. Unless you and your partner take the next step, solving the problem with the Policy of Joint Agreement as your guide, you will remain unhappy. But without an honest expression of feelings, the problem is not even introduced and failure is guaranteed.

Some counselors have encouraged spouses to avoid complaining. Granted, the expression of negative feelings can make intimate conversation very unpleasant if an effort to make an adjustment doesn't immediately follow. But when complaining stops, the hope of an adjustment comes to an end. So complaining isn't the problem—the problem is the partner's failure to address the complaint.

Why does a spouse keep complaining about the same problem again and again? It's because there has been no effort to solve the problem. When a solution is found, the complaining ends.

Your communication of negative reactions should be a two-way street. Honest feelings should be expressed *and* received. Complaints should be heard *and* respected. If you're getting the data, you should read it and then respond to it in a way that reflects your care for your partner. What should be done to resolve the issue? If you react negatively to something that your partner is doing, it's a problem for both of you to solve together.

Persistence is also important. Your commitment to honesty does not end when you have reported a negative feeling once. If that feeling persists, you should continue to express it honestly until the problem is resolved. In other words, for honesty to take place in your relationship, you must allow each other to express negative feelings as they occur, even if they have been expressed in the past. If you often feel lonely, express it often. If your partner offends you, mention it whenever it happens. Keep sending your message until you begin searching for a solution to the problem. There is nothing wrong with the repeated expressions of your negative emotional reactions if the conflict that creates them has not been addressed to your satisfaction.

But there is a difference between expressing your negative emotional reactions until the problem is addressed and nagging: The difference is Love Busters. Nagging involves demands, disrespect, and anger to your honest reactions. If you make demands, express your disrespect, or become angry when your partner does something that bothers you, you will not only fail to solve the problem, but you will also erode your partner's love for you. On the other hand, when you express negative emotional reactions *without* Love Busters, you are simply telling your partner that a problem exists that needs a solution.

Although I've emphasized the difficulty and importance of expressing negative reactions, I don't want to overlook the expression of positive feelings. While positive feelings are generally easier to communicate than negative ones, many couples have not learned to express these feelings either. Failing to do so, they miss an important opportunity to make Love Bank deposits. When your partner does something that makes you feel good, and you communicate that feeling clearly and enthusiastically, you make your partner feel good, knowing that his or her care is appreciated. And your expression of appreciation makes that act of care more likely in the future.

Historical Honesty

Should your skeletons stay in the closet?

Some say "yes": Lock the door, hide the key, and leave well enough alone. Communicate your past misdeeds only on a need-to-know basis.

But if you want to understand each other and make appropriate adjustments, your partner needs to know everything. Whatever embarrassing experiences or serious mistakes are in your past, you should come clean with him or her.

Your personal history holds significant information about you—your strengths and weaknesses. If you want to grow in compatibility, the one you are about to marry should understand both your good and your bad points. When can you be relied on? When do you need help?

For example, if a man has had problems controlling his temper in the past, it's likely he'll have the same struggle in the future. If a woman has been chemically dependent in the past, she'll be susceptible to drug or alcohol abuse in the future. If you talk openly about your past mistakes, your partner will understand your weaknesses, and together you can avoid situations that will tend to create problems for you in the future.

> **Historical Honesty:** Reveal information about your personal history, particularly events that demonstrate personal weakness or failure.

No area of your life should be kept secret from your partner. All questions you ask each other should be answered fully and completely. Give special attention to periods of poor adjustment in your past. Be sure that both you and your partner understand what happened in those previous circumstances. That way you will be able to create a lifestyle together that does not tempt your weaknesses.

Not only should you explain your past to your partner, but you should encourage your partner to gather information from those who knew you before you met. Talk with several significant people from each other's past. Doing so is often quite an eye-opener.

Historical Honesty requires disclosure of any of your past sexual relationships. You should reveal that information because it's among the most important and personal facts that there is to know about you.

"But if I tell her about all the things I've done, she'll never trust me again." "If he finds out about my past, he'll be crushed. It will ruin his whole image of me." I have heard these protests from various clients, all ashamed of things they had done. Why dig it all up? Let old mistakes stay buried in ancient history! Why not just leave those little demons alone? I answer that they're not "little demons" but an extremely important part of the client's personal story.

Some people believe that it's best not to reveal the sins of the past. Why put your partner through the agony of a revelation that could ruin your relationship forever?

There are two answers to that question. The first answer is that your partner has a right to know the truth about you, regardless of the consequences. Even if the facts of your past would cause your partner to reconsider the relationship, he or she deserves to know them.

The second answer is that relationships are ruined not by honesty but by dishonesty. It's far more likely that your partner would consider ending your relationship *after* discovering that you've been dishonest about your past, rather than if you had been honest from the beginning. Furthermore, honesty about the past will help you create precautions to avoid repeating past weaknesses, while dishonesty almost guarantees their intrusion into your relationship.

You may be daunted by the idea of revealing your past, and that's understandable. When you reveal the truth for the first time, there may be a negative reaction and some shaky times in your relationship. But let me assure you that your relationship is likely to be stronger in the long run. Dishonesty destroys intimacy, compatibility, and the feeling of love. Honesty promotes them. I've never witnessed a marriage that was destroyed by honesty.

Although there are no exceptions to the Policy of Radical Honesty, there are some marriages so infected by the Love Buster of angry outbursts that it is not safe to be honest until the threat of abuse is eliminated; honesty may run the risk of a severe beating or even death. In these marriages, I suggest that a couple temporarily separate until safety can be assured. No couple should live together as long as one spouse persists in abusing the other. And if honesty triggers physical or emotional abuse, temporary separation is usually the only reasonable response.

Current Honesty

When couples are engaged, they often share their daily schedules with each other without giving it much thought. But after they are married, many are tempted to neglect this important aspect of honesty.

In good marriages, spouses become so interdependent that sharing a daily schedule is essential to their coordination of activities. In weak marriages, however, spouses are reluctant to reveal their schedules because they often secretly engage in activities that would offend each other if they were known. These spouses hide the details of their day, telling themselves, *What he doesn't know won't hurt him,* or *She's happier not knowing everything.*

Even when activities are innocent, it's extremely important for your partner to know what you do with your time. And since almost everything you do will affect each other, you should discuss your schedules before they are set. Does your schedule make Love Bank deposits or withdrawals?

Current Honesty: Reveal information about the events of your day. Provide your partner with a calendar of your activities, with special emphasis on those that may affect him or her.

Whether there's an emergency or your partner just wants to say hello during the day, be easy to locate. I recommend that you each carry a cell phone whenever you are apart so you make yourselves accessible to each other.

If you follow the Policy of Joint Agreement and the Policy of Radical Honesty, you cannot avoid creating a life of marital compatibility. The two policies work together to prevent the development of harmful habits and encourage a lifestyle that works well for both of you. The Policy of Joint Agreement helps you discover and develop habits and activities that are mutually enjoyable, and the Policy of Radical Honesty prevents you from creating a secret second life where incompatible habits and activities flourish.

Future Honesty

After I've made such a big issue of revealing past indiscretions, you can imagine how I feel about revealing future plans that may get you into trouble. Future plans are much easier to discuss than past mistakes or failures, yet many couples keep their plans secret from each other. Why? Some people believe that communicating future plans just gives a spouse the opportunity to quash them. And other spouses feel that they need to keep a plan secret until they can prove its value. They have their sights set on a certain goal and they don't want anything to stand in their way.

But even if you have only a half-baked plan, why not let your partner know what you're thinking? Why not give your partner an opportunity to think along with you?

When you fail to tell your partner about your plans, you're not being honest. You may be trying to avoid trouble in the present, but eventually the future will arrive, revealing plans that you had kept secret. At that point, your partner will be hurt that you didn't discuss those plans with him or her earlier. Why didn't you take his or her feelings into account when you were making those plans?

Future Honesty: Reveal your thoughts and plans regarding future activities and objectives.

"If I wait for my wife to agree to my plans," a husband might say, "we'll never accomplish anything. She's so conservative; she never wants to take any risks, and so we miss every opportunity that comes along." But don't her feelings mean anything? Isn't this husband forcing his wife to put up with a lifestyle that doesn't fit her? If he cared about her feelings, he would want her input on decisions—he'd want her enthusiastic agreement before putting his plan into action!

"Oh, but the plans I make are best for both of us," a wife might say. "He may not understand my decision now but once he sees how things turn out, he'll thank me for going ahead with it." That's risky reasoning. If he'd thank you later, there's a good chance he'd agree to it now. And if it doesn't turn out as planned, you will not only be blamed for its failure, but your husband will also be very upset with your dishonesty. On the other hand, a plan that is agreed to enthusiastically can fail without draining your Love Bank accounts. Since you both agreed, you both accept responsibility for the failure. And if you can't agree, there's probably a good reason for you to avoid that plan.

There is no good reason to keep plans for the future from each other. Your lifestyle should be created with each other in mind. Neither of you should make independent decisions because everything you plan will affect both of you. Even if your plans work out, your spouse will still feel bad about not being included in the planning.

Complete Honesty

When Myrna and Ronald were dating, they weren't completely honest with each other. Myrna actually had the belief that a little mystery made the relationship better. Ronald believed that some areas of his life deserved to be private.

Eventually, they were married. But their philosophy about honesty didn't change. They continued to hide parts of their lives from each other, giving false impressions about spending, schedule, and computer use. But most importantly, they were giving false impressions about their happiness in marriage. Their lack of complete honesty eventually grew into a monster. Something had to change.

I ask probing questions during premarital counseling. And I probe most deeply into areas where people tend to leave false impressions. Since most marital problems originate with serious misconceptions, I try to dig out these little weeds that eventually choke the plant.

False impressions are just as deceitful as outright lies. The purpose of honesty is to have the facts in front of you. Without them, you'll fail to solve the simplest marital problems. Whether you lie to your spouse or give a false impression, you're leaving him or her ignorant of the facts.

> **Complete Honesty:** Do not leave your partner with a false impression about your thoughts, feelings, habits, likes, dislikes, personal history, daily activities, or plans for the future. Do not deliberately keep any personal information from your partner.

In marriage, one of the biggest false impressions I find is that both spouses are doing an outstanding job meeting each other's needs.

This form of deceit is often particularly tempting early in a relationship. These are some areas in which one or both of you are dissatisfied, but you don't want to appear unappreciative. You don't want to run the risk of losing your relationship by expressing your dissatisfaction.

That concern is understandable. But you can minimize that risk by expressing your concerns in ways that are nonthreatening or nonjudgmental. You can show appreciation for the effort made to meet your needs and then provide guidance to make that effort more effective.

Only the true expression of your feelings will help you find solutions to the problems you face. You cripple your relationship whenever you do not reveal the complete truth. Honesty provides the only map that leads to marital success.

Again, if you and your spouse have trouble controlling Love Busters when honesty is revealed, I recommend that you read Dr. Harley's book, *Love Busters* (Harley, 1992, 2016), or if needed, seek professional help immediately to ensure a zero-tolerance for your own Love Busters. Also, to help you with honesty, you may want to download and use *The Gift of Honesty* mobile app, and E^2: *Explore and Engage* mobile app from FourGiftsofLove.org, Google Play, and Apple App Store (*The Gift of Honesty* app helps you create and send a text using the phrase *I'd love it if*, *I love it when*, and 1-5 rating scale; E^2 offers conversation starters that combine original-photographic images with thought-provoking questions to spark the gift of honesty).

Remember, honesty is never your enemy; it's a friend that brings light to problems that often need a creative solution. If honesty is followed by safe and pleasant negotiation, it becomes the necessary first step toward improving your compatibility and love for each other.

Review

1. Don't make your partner miserable when he or she tells you the truth. Instead of trying to punish your partner when a shocking truth is revealed, reward the honesty. To help couples do this, they learn to say, "Thank you for being honest." If they feel that they need time to process the new information to protect their spouse from any Love Buster, they add, "Can I have X minutes to think about this and then we'll get back together to talk about it?" If honesty is followed by safe and pleasant negotiation, it becomes the necessary first step toward improving your compatibility and love for each other. It is important to create an environment where you can work together to achieve greater love and compatibility.

2. Dishonesty creates mistrust and insecurity. Dishonesty has at least three important negative consequences: 1) feelings are hurt when dishonesty is discovered; 2) misinformation causes adjustment to the wrong target; and 3) an important emotional need is not met (honesty). Dishonesty is also short-sighted—getting what you want now and dealing with the consequences later helps create habits that you will repeat until you're caught.

3. Honesty creates understanding and emotional bonding. Honesty helps you protect your spouse from potentially harmful habits.

Thought Questions

1. When do you think dishonesty with your spouse is justified?

2. What do you think about "white lies"? Is it sometimes difficult to tell the truth? What situations are harder and why?

3. Do you see how false impressions are a form of deceit that could damage a marriage?

22

Understanding Dishonesty

You have undoubtedly discussed the subject of honesty with each other and have probably agreed to be honest throughout your lives together. That's what most couples do. That's what Joyce and I did when we were first married. In fact, it was so important to us that we created a way to avoid any misunderstanding. If either of us asked the other the question "On your word?" it meant no joking. The other person had to tell the truth. We still follow that rule today.

But as much as couples want an honest relationship, there are four important reasons that dishonesty sneaks into marriages: 1) protection; 2) avoiding trouble; 3) looking better than you are; and 4) compulsion. While the excuses are very different for each type of dishonesty, the result is the same—the marriage suffers.

Lying to Protect

The most common type of dishonesty in marriage is motivated by protection. It hurts to be criticized, so spouses often avoid expressing their negative feelings toward each other, because they don't want to hurt each other. In other cases, people may protect their spouses from unpleasant information, perhaps a health scare or a financial setback.

I call these people *protector liars,* and most of us fit this category, at least once in a while. Almost all of us can think of times when we have withheld our true feelings or the complete truth to avoid upsetting someone.

It seems quite innocent, doesn't it? Why upset your partner? Why ruin his or her good mood? But when you are being dishonest to protect your partner's feelings, you're actually *denying* your partner crucial information. How would you feel if your bank stopped giving you monthly statements on your checking account but deducted fees without informing you? You'd be outraged. "When our customers run low in their accounts," the bank manager might say, "we try to protect them from that unpleasant information." That would be crazy! That's exactly when you *need* information, so you can make a deposit and avoid bouncing checks.

The same is true for you and your partner. You need to know when you are making Love Bank withdrawals so you can make adjustments to prevent further loss. Without that information, you risk blindly drifting into Love Bank insolvency.

When you are experiencing negative feelings for your partner, you must let him or her know that withdrawals are taking place. That's the first step toward making the adjustments necessary to plug the leak in your Love Bank.

And when unpleasant financial or health information comes to your attention, why keep it from your partner? Do you have so little confidence in your partner that you don't believe he or she can handle it? That's not only disrespectful, but it also prevents you from benefiting from the wisdom your partner has to offer.

Neither of you need protection from the facts. They are the friends of wise solutions. If you both share the facts you know with each other, and respect each other's judgment, you will find that you'll be wiser together than you could have ever been separately.

Lying to Avoid Trouble

The second most common type of dishonesty in marriage is motivated by avoiding trouble. I call these dishonest people *avoiding-trouble liars*. They do things they know would upset their spouse—if they were revealed. So they deny doing them. Lies of this nature can be devastating to a marriage because they help create a secret second life that is totally incompatible with the feelings and interests of the other spouse. Almost all of a marriage's most destructive habits grow in the hothouse of secret second lives—infidelity, drug and alcohol addiction, sexual addiction, and gambling, to name a few.

Having owned and operated chemical dependency treatment centers in the past, I am very impressed with the lengths addicts will go to keep their addiction secret. One man I counseled kept his wife in the dark about his alcohol abuse by keeping gin in a windshield washer container, using blue food coloring to make it look  authentic. She was completely fooled until the day he ran into the house grabbing at his throat and demanding that she rush him to the nearest emergency room. Unbeknown to him, his uncle had used his bottle of gin as windshield washer the day before, and came back the next day to replace it with the real thing. Once the secret was revealed, he voluntarily entered treatment and has been sober ever since.

The first step of recovery from a host of addictions is to expose them to the light of day. Most addicts would all live healthier and happier lives if their family and friends all knew everything they did. If someone with a video camera were to follow them around, they would be far less tempted to engage in self-destructive addictive behavior. But it's particularly important for their spouse to know what they do. It helps them overcome addiction and also helps keep them from forming those habits in the first place.

But it's not just addictive behavior that can be avoided by being honest; it's anything that would create incompatibility in marriage.

As we saw earlier, compatibility is created by following the Policy of Joint Agreement whenever decisions are made. If partners make decisions with each other's feelings and interests in mind, they create a lifestyle that benefits both of them. On the other hand, if they make decisions independently of each other, their drift into incompatibility is assured.

How can the Policy of Joint Agreement be followed if spouses are not honest about every aspect of their lives? "What my spouse doesn't know won't hurt him (or her)," is simply not true. If you secretly practice behavior that would offend your spouse when revealed, that behavior can turn into habits that can be very difficult to overcome. What begins as an occasional diversion can eventually become so much a part of your life that it dominates you. By the time it's revealed, it would seem almost impossible to stop.

That's one of the most important reasons that the Policy of Joint Agreement and the Policy of Radical Honesty should be followed throughout marriage. If you are honest about all of your activities and avoid any that you can't agree on, habits that are the most difficult to overcome will never gain a foothold. One of a couple's greatest struggles in marriage is trying to create compatibility after having created independent lifestyles. But you can avoid those lifestyles and never have to face that struggle in the first place by following these two policies.

You should be transparent with each other. A secret second life, separate from the scrutiny of your spouse, should not exist in your marriage. Almost everything you do, even what you do in private, will affect each other, so do everything with each other in mind. And never lie about something you did if it would not have been approved by your spouse. Lying to cover up a violation of the Policy of Joint Agreement deals a double blow from the lying spouse— failing to protect and failing to be honest.

Lying to Look Better than You Are

Those I call the *looking-better-than-you-are liars* are found mostly on first dates. But enough end up getting married to become the third most common type of dishonest spouse. As is also the case with avoiding-trouble liars, these people get away with lying for a while because they usually demand the right to privacy, and their spouse obliges them. Privacy has no place in marriage, and those who express offense when their spouse checks up on them are likely candidates for all forms of dishonesty. A husband comes home from work beaming. He tells his wife that he's just been given an award for being the best salesman at the office—the fourth award given to him this year. His wife never asks for evidence, such as a raise, or even a certificate describing the award. Instead, she congratulates him. He thinks, *What harm is there in giving her the impression that I'm a very successful husband?*

The harm, of course, is that he is misrepresenting himself to her, and that has devastating consequences in marriage. Most men want to be admired by their wives, but admiration based on lies sets him up for a spectacular fall. When she finally discovers that he's been deceitful, she loses not only the false respect she had for a man she thought was very successful, but she loses *all* respect for him. After all, a man who has to lie to gain the respect of his wife is pathetic.

Never exaggerate your accomplishments. Instead, provide factual, accurate, and documented information so that your spouse knows with certainty that you are telling the truth. And if he or she wants more proof, don't express resentment—just cheerfully provide the evidence that's requested.

If you have ever lied to your partner, expect a certain degree of skepticism until trust is restored. You can speed up that restoration by treating that skepticism with respect. If instead, you demand trust of your partner and are offended whenever he or she wants evidence for a statement you've made, you will keep your partner in a state of distrust indefinitely.

Lying Compulsively

The fourth type of dishonest spouse, and the least common, is the compulsive liar. These people lie about anything and everything, whether they have a good reason or not. I call them *born liars*. They don't seem to be able to control their lying, nor do they know why they do it. They often lie about personal experiences and accomplishments, and sometimes even convince themselves that the lies are true. Even evidence to the contrary does not always dissuade them.

Born liars often lead double lives. They are sometimes married to more than one person at once. They may pass themselves off as doctors or lawyers, and get away with it, in spite of their lack of formal background. When caught in their crime, they sincerely deny any guilt and can even pass lie detector tests. Such liars are fascinating to psychologists like me but, for obvious reasons, are impossible as marriage partners. Since honesty is essential in marriage and these individuals simply cannot tell the truth, their marriages are almost always very short-lived.

How do they get away with it? These imposters often masquerade for years before they're exposed. The answer to that question is that too many people respect their privacy. They simply fail to look into their background. You have every right to obtain corroborating evidence for information you receive from each other. And if your partner objects to such scrutiny, then I suggest you search even more diligently.

Is Honesty a Love Buster

Isn't honesty, in some cases, a Love Buster? Are there times when a couple can be *too* honest with each other, when it would be better to avoid conflict by keeping a spouse in the dark?

That's what many couples think. They assume their relationship would suffer harm if they expressed their true feelings. On the surface, this argument seems to make sense. Love Busters are those actions that make your spouse unhappy; so if your expression of honesty troubles your spouse, isn't it a Love Buster?

Actually, it's not. When you take a closer look, you find that the Love Buster in such a situation isn't honesty itself, but the behavior the honesty reveals. For example, confessing to an affair will certainly upset your spouse. But it isn't the confession that's upsetting, it's the affair!

In most cases, dishonesty merely postpones your spouse's discovery of the truth, and once it's revealed, the fact that you lied will do even more damage to your relationship. Then your spouse will be upset by the truth *and* by your dishonesty. And of the two, your dishonesty will usually hurt your spouse more than whatever it was you were trying to conceal. Dishonesty in marriage, once discovered, causes incredible pain.

Don't Wrap Your Honesty in Love Busters

While honesty is never a Love Buster itself, it can serve as a disguise for true Love Busters. Consider this: Someday you may have difficulty making a sexual adjustment. In frustration, you may finally blurt out, "We've gone two weeks, and I've heard enough excuses. It's time!" There's nothing wrong with an honest appeal for help, but if it turns out to be a demand, it's a Love Buster. Instead of expressing your need and encouraging your spouse to meet that need, you make yourself repulsive. Don't demand what you need from each other; request it with respect. That way, your need will be heard and responded to favorably.

Or, instead of making demands, you say, "Your priorities are certainly screwed up. You seem to think that money is more important than I am. If you don't straighten out soon, you'll be sleeping with your money." Again, that may be your honest opinion, but it's also a disrespectful judgment that will put your spouse on the defensive. As a result, he or she never really hears what you're saying. Whatever is gained by expressing your feelings is quickly lost in the Love Buster.

Or, imagine expressing your unhappiness by throwing a lamp and crying out, "You never have time for me anymore. I don't know why I ever married you, you selfish jerk!" The fact that you were trying to communicate—that you want your spouse to spend more time with you—is completely lost in your angry outburst. You're not communicating when your spouse is running for cover.

It's often not easy to express feelings while keeping selfish demands, disrespectful judgments, or angry outbursts in check. Anyone can learn to do it, though.

"If you don't start spending more time with me soon, I'll find someone else to spend time with" is a selfish demand. "I'd like to spend more time with you" is an honest statement of feeling.

"I'm the least important person in your life. You'd rather be with anyone else but me" is a disrespectful judgment because you are telling your spouse how he or she feels. The truth is you don't know how your spouse feels unless he or she tells you. "I become upset when I'm left alone at night" is an honest statement of your feeling, because you are telling your spouse how *you* feel.

If you are to be honest with your spouse, you must be willing to reveal your feelings, but in a way that helps your marriage and doesn't hurt your marriage. Demands, disrespect, and anger will always hurt your marriage. Honesty without those Love Busters will always help.

Encourage Each Other to Be Honest

You may say that you want your spouse to be honest, but your values and reactions may not encourage honesty. How do you answer the following questions?

1. If the truth would be terribly upsetting to you, do you want your partner to be honest with you only at times when you are emotionally prepared?

2. Do you keep some aspects of your life secret? Do you encourage your partner to respect your privacy or boundaries in those areas?

3. Do you like to create a certain mystery between you and your partner?

4. Are there conditions under which you would not want honesty at all costs between you and your partner?

If you answer "yes" to any of these questions, you fail to send a clear message that you want an honest relationship. In certain situations, you feel your marriage is better off with dishonesty, or at least with something less than the truth. That little crack is all dishonesty needs to slip into your marriage and eventually run amok. You see, there are always "reasons" to be dishonest. As soon as you allow one, they begin to blur into all the rest, and before you know it, you have a dishonest relationship.

You encourage honesty when you *value* honesty. If your own values do not consistently support honesty, you will be sending each other mixed messages that will undermine this third gift.

Having consistent values is one way to encourage honesty. Another important way is in the way you react to honesty. Do your reactions convey an appreciation for the truth, even if it's painful? These questions will help you determine if you are actually discouraging honesty in the way you sometimes react to it.

1. Do you ever make selfish demands when your partner is honest with you?

2. Do you ever make disrespectful judgments when your partner is honest with you?

3. Do you ever have angry outbursts when your partner is honest with you?

If you answered "yes" to any of these questions, you are using Love Busters to punish honesty and are inadvertently encouraging dishonesty. The way to encourage each other to be truthful is to minimize the negative consequences of truthful revelations. Instead of trying to punish your partner when truth is revealed, try to reward your partner's honesty. Remember, honesty itself is never your enemy: It's a friend that brings light to a problem that often needs a creative solution. If honesty is followed by safe and pleasant negotiation, it becomes the necessary first step toward improvement in your compatibility and love for each other.

When you are on the receiving end of an honest disclosure, you come face-to-face with how difficult it is to reward honesty. When faced with the truth, some spouses react with rage. Some cry, some scream, some hit, some threaten—and all these reactions tend to encourage dishonesty in the future. Don't make your partner miserable when he or she tells you the truth. Instead, tell your partner, "Thank you for being honest with me." Then discuss ways that you can work together to achieve greater love and compatibility.

Review

- Dishonesty creates mistrust and insecurity. Dishonesty has at least three important negative consequences:

  1. Feelings are hurt when dishonesty is discovered.
  2. Misinformation causes adjustment to the wrong target.
  3. An important emotional need is not met (honesty and openness).

- Dishonesty is also short-sighted—getting what you want now and dealing with the consequences later helps create habits that you will repeat until you're caught.

- Honesty creates understanding and emotional bonding. Honesty helps you protect your partner from potentially harmful habits.

- Don't make your partner miserable when he or she tells you the truth. Create an environment where you can work together to achieve greater love and compatibility.

Thought Questions

1. If you find yourself lying, or misrepresenting the truth, is it most often to protect others or to avoid trouble?

2. Do your values encourage the habit of honesty? Ask yourself these questions:
   - If the truth would be terribly upsetting to you, would you still want to be told the truth?
   - Do you feel that there is no room for privacy in marriage?
   - Should you try to take the mystery out of your relationship? Do you want honesty under all circumstances?

3. Do your reactions to honesty encourage the habit of honesty? Ask yourself these questions:
   o Do you avoid selfish demands when your partner is honest?
   o Do you avoid disrespectful judgments when your partner is honest?
   o Do you avoid angry outbursts when your partner is honest?

P.S. The way to encourage each other to be truthful is to minimize the negative consequences of truthful revelations. Instead of trying to punish your partner when a shocking truth is revealed, try to reward the honesty. To help couples do this, I have them learn to say, **"Thank you for being honest."** If they feel they need some time to process the new information, to protect their spouse from any Love Buster, I have them add, "Can I have ten minutes to think about this, and then we'll get back together to talk about it?" If honesty is followed by safe and pleasant negotiation, it becomes the necessary first step toward improving your compatibility and love for each other.

PART FOUR

The Gift of Time

I PROMISE TO
SCHEDULE TIME TO
GIVE YOU MY
UNDIVIDED ATTENTION

23

The Gift of Time with God

D o you remember your first job? Mine was working at a specialty food store in a mall selling cheese and sweeping the floor. I vividly remember my excitement every Friday afternoon when the next week's schedule was posted. I took my evening job very seriously and all other events were scheduled around that job.

But what would have happened if I hadn't taken the schedule seriously? What if I had gone to work only when I felt like it or when I had nothing better to do? The answer is obvious—I would have been fired and would have failed to achieve my goal of earning money for college.

Most of us have a detailed schedule for work, exercise, education, special appointments, or sport activities. Some even own special electronic devices or calendars to list these important events in their lives. We are highly motivated to make schedules for these events because without setting aside this time, our commitments wouldn't be kept and our goals wouldn't be achieved.

Similarly, what would happen if we say to God and to our spouse, "I'll spend time with you if I have nothing better to do—after I've done everything else that's scheduled"? The answer is obvious again—your promise to love and cherish would not be fulfilled and those important relationships would suffer neglect.

When it comes to scheduling time with God and a spouse, many find this concept strange. They're familiar with scheduling everything else in their lives, but not this. Even though their dating relationship was scheduled, they feel that after they're married scheduling is unnecessary. After all, they're with each other when they sleep! Isn't that enough time? And God is with them all the time. Why should they schedule time to be with someone who's always there? As a result, many find themselves giving these most important relationships their "left-over" time.

Part Four is dedicated to help you keep your promises to God and to your spouse by making sure they have your best time—not your left-over time. Otherwise, you'll neglect both of them.

In the following chapters, you will have an opportunity to create the habit of scheduling quality time with your partner—allowing you to give your gifts of care, protection, and honesty. And this chapter will help you achieve your promise-fulfilling goals to love and cherish God by creating a plan to set aside quality time with Him.

So, let's get started. Here is a sample plan for you to try or you can develop your own plan.

Sample Plan: Identify regular times during the day to pause, talk, and listen to God.

1. Schedule three, five-minute periods of time spaced throughout each day (e.g., after each meal or at other specified times during the day). During each of these time segments, worship Him and give Him your gift of honesty:

   a. Reflect on who God is
   b. Give praises to God in recognition of who He is
   c. Confess the sinful behavior you have done since your last 5-minutes with Him

    d. Give thanks

    e. Tell Him your concerns and ask for what you desire

2. After one week, add the following to the plan: At each specified time, also reflect on how close your fellowship was during the three or four preceding hours. How much of the time was He outside, knocking at your door? Were you increasing your awareness of God's incredible care and love for you? Were you sensitive to His leading—asking, "What would Jesus do?" when making decisions? Then pledge to maintain close fellowship with Him during the next three or four hours.

3. Over a period of time, make an effort to increase the frequency of your personal contact with God between the three specified times during the day. Intervals with no contact would become shorter and you would become more sensitive to them. Eventually, your continual fellowship with God would be a habit, a very basic, but essential part of your lifestyle.

4. Your goal is to do what you read in 1 Thessalonians 5:17-18: "Pray without ceasing; in everything give thanks; for this is God's will for you in Christ Jesus." This means keeping regular and open communication with God—giving Him your gift of time.

People who have used this plan to improve their time with God have reported, at first, that they run out of things to say in one or two minutes. Their prayer life has been so poor that it was like talking to a stranger. But after about a week, they find themselves spending more and more time in deep and meaningful fellowship with God.

After practicing this plan for one month, you will probably find that giving this gift has become a habit. You will not find it at all difficult to spend time with God throughout your day.

But the result of this plan doesn't only give God your gift of time. The result also gives *you* a gift. During these times with God, His Spirit has your attention and is able to guide you in His will. Being in regular contact with God will open your eyes to His presence in your life. With regular time, you will see His hand working around you and with you, and you will feel His presence and comfort more than ever before.

God is the most wonderful Person you will ever know. He is kind to you. He wants the very best for you. He loves you very much. His personality is infallible and He is the most consistent Friend you will ever have! When all of your other friends are gone, He will still be with you. The *more* you know Him, the *more* you will love Him!

Action Step: For the next three days, keep a daily log of the time you spend with God. Then create a plan on how you can increase that time with Him on a daily basis.

Thought Questions

1. Luke 10:38-42 tells us about a time when Jesus visited the home of two women, Mary and Martha. Mary sat at her Lord's feet and listened to His teaching, while Martha continued her hospitality and hostess duties. Jesus clearly expressed which woman's behavior pleased Him saying, "Martha, Martha…you are worried and upset about many things, but few things are needed—or indeed only one.

Mary has chosen what is better, and it will not be taken away from her" (vs. 41-42 NIV). Is your life like Martha's life; preoccupied with so many distractions (some even God-honoring, like Martha's care for her guests) that you don't find the time to talk with Jesus?

2. Or is your life like Mary's life: prioritized with setting aside the seemingly infinite and necessary tasks of life so you can have time with the most valuable One in your life?

P.S. Scheduling time with God should be easier than scheduling time with your partner because giving God the gift of time doesn't depend on coordinating two schedules—it only depends on yours. Jesus said, "And behold, I am with you always, to the end of the age" (Matthew 28:20b). Jesus promised to always be available to you through the Holy Spirit—24 hours, 7 days a week.

Isn't that fact amazing? He is always available. God is there for you during the most hectic traffic jam, in the incredibly long line at the store, during the greatest joys in life and the greatest sorrows.

But God doesn't force you to spend time with Him. And He doesn't schedule your time. We read in Revelation 3:20, "Here I am! I stand at the door and knock. If anyone hears My voice and opens the door, I will come in and eat with him, and he with Me." Your Lord stands at the door of each moment of your life, waiting to be invited in.

Remember, spending time with God is never a waste. It is a time when He can care for you. If you let Him into your happiness, He will rejoice with you. If you let Him into your pain, He will comfort you and give you peace. He is available to you always. You just need to carve out time for Him—give Him the gift of time as He perfectly gives you the gift of time.

24
The Gift of Time

⁜

Ask anyone and they'd tell you that Sherry and Joe have "hearts of gold." Even with two full-time jobs and a 2-year-old daughter, Mary, they always find time to nurture their friendships and offer help when needed.

One friend, who Joe had helped, decided to give them a weekend vacation at a beach resort. Although Sherry was a little apprehensive about leaving Mary behind for the two nights, she agreed.

The weekend arrived. Sherry and Joe had a beautiful ocean view right outside of their very secluded beach bungalow. But there was a problem: "What are we going to do with all of this time together?" they each privately thought. Their lives were so filled with work and caring for others that they had forgotten how to enjoy being alone, just the two of them. It was actually an uncomfortable feeling.

During that weekend, Joe and Sherry realized something wasn't right. They didn't "fit together" like they did when they were first married. And the truth was that they didn't enjoy each other's company. They had become incompatible.

Thankfully, they were honest with each other and talked about it. They were able to identify the main variable that changed in their life: Their time was not prioritized correctly. Their most important human relationship was in last place. This was a major revelation that led to a radical change in their schedule.

The gifts of care, protection, and honesty are easily understood as essential for marital health and happiness. They're not always given regularly in marriage, however, most of us know deep down, that they *should* be given.

But there is still one more gift that you and your partner should present to each other. It's not only more difficult to understand as essential for marital happiness, it's also more difficult to give than the other three. It is the gift of time.

The Gift of Time: The gift of time is a willingness and effort to give undivided attention, using it to provide the most meaningful acts of care for the other.

Most engaged couples try to talk to each other every day. If they can't physically be with each other, they talk on the telephone, sometimes for hours. And when they are together, they are probably very affectionate with each other. Hugs and kisses abound. They are also likely to spend the majority of their recreational time together. And that time they spend talking to each other, being affectionate, and enjoying recreational activities together is the best part of their week. They look forward to it more than anything else they do.

For these couples, time together isn't determined by chance. Since it's their highest priority, they carefully fit each other into their schedules and may even cancel other plans so that they can be together more often. That's because they want to be with each other as often as possible.

But let's suppose for a moment that these engaged couples didn't plan their time together. Instead, they would talk to each other, express their affection, and enjoy recreational activities together only when they both had nothing else to do. If that were the case, they probably wouldn't be together very often. And they probably wouldn't be getting married either.

My research on common dating practices helped me come to that conclusion. Most couples with marriage on their mind tend to give each other their undivided attention at least fifteen hours each week. These results should not be surprising since it takes quite a bit of time to meet the most important emotional needs. And those needs must be met to trigger and sustain the feeling of romantic love.

In fact, one reason people marry is to spend even more time together. But unless they promise each other their time, they will find that after they are married, they will not be giving each other *more* undivided attention; they'll be giving each other *less*! That's because most couples think being together physically is the same as being together emotionally. They may actually spend more time together after marriage, but they will not necessarily be using that time to meet each other's most important emotional needs.

Before marriage, being together physically usually means you are also together emotionally. But after marriage, you may find that you can be in the same room together and yet ignore each other emotionally. Even worse, you may find that you are not even in the same room together as much as you had expected to be, particularly after your children arrive.

One of the most difficult aspects of marriage counseling is finding time in a couple's schedule for it. The counselor must often work evenings and weekends because most couples will not give up their time at work for their appointments. And the counselor must also schedule around a host of evening and weekend activities that take the husband and wife in opposite directions.

But the problem of finding time for the couple's counseling appointment is almost insignificant compared to the problem of finding time to carry out their first assignment. And that's especially true when—as I instruct my clients—their first week's assignment is to give each other fifteen hours of their undivided attention. Many couples think that their problems will be solved with a weekly conversation in the counselor's office. It doesn't occur to them that it's what they do after they leave the office that saves their marriage.

It's incredible how many couples have tried to talk me out of their spending more time together. They begin by trying to convince me that it's impossible. Then they go on to the argument that it's impractical. But in the end, they usually agree that without time they cannot possibly re-create the love they once had for each other.

To prevent you from making the common mistake of neglecting each other after marriage or to help you recover from getting off track, I suggest that you follow The Policy of Undivided Attention.

> **The Policy of Undivided Attention:** Give your spouse your undivided attention a minimum of fifteen hours each week, using the time to meet his or her emotional needs of affection, sexual fulfillment, intimate conversation, and recreational companionship.

This policy has three important corollary rules that help explain how it is to be followed.

Corollary 1: Privacy. The time you plan to be together should not include children, relatives, or friends. Establish privacy so that you are able to give each other your undivided attention.

It's essential that, as a couple, you spend time alone. When you have time alone, you have a much greater opportunity to give each other undivided attention, and it takes undivided attention to meet the most intimate emotional needs.

First, I recommend that you learn to be together without children present. This is an easy assignment if you don't yet have children of your own. But it will be much more difficult after children have arrived. Many couples don't think children interfere with their privacy. To them, an evening with their children *is* privacy. Of course, they know they can't make love with children around. But I believe that the presence of children prevents much more than lovemaking. When children are present, they interfere with affection and intimate conversation which are essential ingredients for a happy marriage.

Second, I recommend that friends and relatives not be present during your time together. This may mean that after everything has been scheduled, there's no time left over for friends and relatives. If that's the case, you're too busy, but at least you won't be sacrificing your love for each other.

Third, I recommend that you remember why you are together: for undivided attention. It's what you did while dating. You planned to marry because you looked at each other when you were talking, you were interested in the conversation, and there was little to distract you. This is the undivided attention you should continue to give each other as a married couple.

When you see a movie together, it shouldn't count toward your time for undivided attention unless you're being affectionate throughout the movie. The same applies to watching television or sporting events. Don't stop doing these things together, but count them as time for undivided attention only when you pay close attention to each other.

Now that you're alone with each other, what should you do with this time? The second corollary of the Policy of Undivided Attention deals with objectives.

Corollary 2: Objectives. *During the time you are together as a married couple, focus on meeting the emotional needs of affection, sexual fulfillment, intimate conversation, and recreational companionship.*

For most husbands, romance is sex and recreation; for most wives, it's affection and intimate conversation. When all four come together, husbands and wives alike call it romance, and they deposit the most love units possible. That makes these four categories somewhat inseparable whenever you spend time together. My advice is to try to do them all when you give each other undivided attention.

Unfortunately, most couples are tempted to take shortcuts. A wife often tries to get her husband to meet the emotional needs for intimate conversation and affection, without necessarily meeting his needs for sex and recreational companionship. A husband, on the other hand, usually wants his wife to meet his needs for sexual fulfillment and recreational companionship, without meeting her needs for affection and intimate conversation. As you may imagine, neither shortcut works very well. Women often resent having sex without affection and intimate conversation, while men resent being attentive and affectionate with no hope for sexual fulfillment or recreational companionship. By combining the four into a single event, however, both spouses have their needs met and enjoy their time together.

A man should never assume that just because he is in bed with his wife, sex is there for his taking. In many new marriages, that mistake creates resentment and confusion. But if a husband spends the evening giving his wife his undivided attention, with intimate conversation and affection, sex becomes a very natural and mutually enjoyable way to end the evening.

The flip side of this is also true, and women need to see that connection. If a woman wants her husband to give her the most attention when there is no possibility for sex, she'll leave him frustrated most of the time. Knowing that affection and intimate conversation often lead a man to desire sex, some women try their hardest to be affectionate when they are out in a crowd. That tactic can lead to just as much resentment in a man as a nightly sexual "ambush" creates in a woman. Take my word for it: The fulfillment of the four needs of affection, intimate conversation, recreational companionship, and sexual fulfillment is best when they are met together.

Corollary 3: Amount. *The number of hours to be together should reflect the quality of your marriage. If your marriage is satisfying to you and your spouse, schedule fifteen hours each week for your undivided attention. But if you suffer marital dissatisfaction in your marriage, plan more time until marital satisfaction is achieved.*

How much time do you need to sustain the feeling of romantic love? Believe it or not, there really is an answer to this question, and it depends on the health of a marriage. If a couple is deeply in love with each other and finds that their marital needs are being met, I have found that about fifteen hours each week of undivided attention is usually enough to sustain romantic love. It is probably the least amount of time necessary. When a marriage is this healthy, either it's a new marriage or the couple has already been spending fifteen hours a week alone with each other throughout their marriage.

As I mentioned in Corollary 2, I usually recommend scheduling enough time to meet all four emotional needs. That's usually three to four hours for each date. Spouses not only require that much time to meet those needs, but they also require it to become emotionally connected when they are together.

If you're wondering how you're supposed to find all this time for undivided attention when you are already juggling commitments of careers, home maintenance, and other responsibilities, think about this: How does a workaholic businessperson find time to have an affair? The man or woman who couldn't be home for dinner because of a busy schedule is suddenly able to fit in midafternoon rendezvous three times a week. But how does the work get done when they do this? The answer, of course, is that there was time all along. It's simply a matter of priorities. The workaholic could just as easily have taken the time with his or her spouse. Then they would have been in love with each other. Instead, he or she creates the feeling of romantic love for someone else, all because of a shortsighted schedule.

The reason I have so much difficulty getting couples to spend time alone together is that most couples I counsel are not in love. Their relationship doesn't do anything for them, and the time spent with each other seems like a total waste at first. But without that time, they have no hope of restoring the love they had for each other. And after meeting each other's most important emotional needs for a while, they want to spend more than fifteen hours together each week. They're in love again.

However, even couples in love can find reasons to avoid time for undivided attention. After being married for a while, most couples find time slipping away as pressure increases to use it for added household responsibilities, childcare, and income. They feel that they don't have time to meet each other's emotional needs when these new pressures strike.

You will also be tempted to stop taking the time to meet each other's intimate emotional needs. But don't do it. Your time together is too important to the security of your relationship and of your children. Remember, the time it takes to stay in love with each other is equivalent to only a part-time job. It isn't time you don't have; it's time you will use for something far less important if you don't use it for each other.

Action Step: For the next three days keep a daily log of the time you spend together as a couple.

Talk About This:

1. When you spend time together as a married couple, why should you focus on four particular needs? What are they?

2. If you could have incredible wealth or success in your career but would have to work long hours that keep you from spending daily time with your spouse, would you do it? What would be the cost?

3. How would you feel if your partner prioritized the time with you as being of lesser importance than career, recreational activity, children, or friends?

4. What part of the gift of time will be the most challenging for you to protect (privacy, objectives, amount)? Do you have any ideas for how to protect those important parts?

5. Temptations for your time will abound in your life together. What would tempt you to schedule less than fifteen hours each week for undivided attention? Financial pressures? Career requirements? Children's needs? Personal goals? Whatever prevents you from giving each other your undivided attention throughout your lives together is a threat to your love for each other and your marriage. What can you do to resist those temptations?

6. Can you make the following commitment to each other? Before making each major decision in life, think about how it could affect giving each other the gift of time.

25

Scheduling Time for Undivided Attention

A fter their "weekend-beach revelation," Joe and Sherry started to make more time for each other. Joe recommended that they go out for dinner the next weekend to start their new plan. The night arrived and Sherry was thrilled to be alone with Joe for this romantic dinner date.

Suddenly Joe's cell phone rings, and he talks for five minutes. Soon Sherry begins to feel frustrated. After he apologizes and they restart their interrupted conversation, Sherry gets a text that "needs" an immediate response. Their lack of undivided attention sadly destroyed their date.

This scene illustrates what can happen to marriages these days. Joe and Sherry thought they were getting credit for spending time with each other. But because they failed to give each other undivided attention, they failed to meet each other's emotional needs; all it did was infer that they were not as important as the next phone call or text. As Joe and Sherry started to add more time in their schedule for each other, they realized that they still had habits that conflicted with their new marriage philosophy.

As soon as you marry, and especially after you have children, obstacles appear that make it seemingly impossible to give each other the undivided attention that you both need. You will find that as your life becomes more complex, you will try to accomplish several objectives at once, and when you spend time together, you will be thinking of other pressing problems that need your attention.

The longer you're married, the busier you will become. You will not be able to do everything you want to do. And if you are not careful, the things that are most important to you will get pushed aside by things that are less important but seem more urgent.

That's what makes a schedule so important. It helps you determine how you will spend your week before urgent demands start to pile up. Instead of mindlessly attending to every demand, you can decide what is most valuable to you in advance, and then decline to do what's less important.

Imagine having a lawn-mowing service that is so popular that people constantly call to have you care for their yards. But because so many people call, you never have a chance to get out of the house to mow any lawns. Regardless of the number of calls you get, you are unable to earn a living because you never leave the phone. It's always ringing, and you feel you must be there to answer it.

You can get just as sidetracked in your marriage. Just as a lawn-mowing business will go broke if you're too busy to mow any lawns, the love in your marriage will be lost if you don't have time to meet each other's intimate emotional needs. If you don't protect your time together, you will find that responsibilities of lesser value will fill it up.

Scheduling Your Time for Undivided Attention

Your love for each other cannot be created or sustained without time for undivided attention. And unless you schedule time to meet each other's intimate emotional needs, it won't get done. As I mentioned earlier, setting aside time to give each other undivided attention will become the most difficult promise to keep, not because you will object to being with each other, but because the pressures of life will tempt you to crowd out the time it takes to sustain your romantic love.

Learn now to schedule at least fifteen hours a week for undivided attention. Get into the habit of sitting down together once a week (for example, 3:30 on Sunday afternoon) to decide when you will be together and how you plan to spend that time. Since we are creatures of habit, I recommend that the hours you spend alone together be at the same time, week after week. If you keep the same schedule every week, it will be easier to follow the Policy of Undivided Attention.

Action Step: Determine a regular meeting time to plan your time together each week. Schedule fifteen hours this week to follow the Policy of Undivided Attention.

The total amount of time you spend together doesn't necessarily affect the way you feel about each other in the week that the time is spent. It has more of an effect on the way you're *going to feel* about each other in future weeks. If you miss a few weeks of undivided attention, you will probably still feel in love, but your Love Bank balances will have started to drop. And if you continue to neglect time together, you may not even notice when those balances fall below the romantic love threshold—until you do spend time together trying to meet each other's intimate emotional needs. You'll find that doing so is much more difficult when you're not in love.

That's why so many couples never do restore their love for each other after they've neglected each other's emotional needs for a while—it seems too awkward and insincere. The romantic love that helped make it easy is gone.

But any couple can rebuild their Love Bank accounts if they meet each other's intimate emotional needs, even when it feels awkward to do so. Eventually, their Love Bank balances rise above the romantic love threshold, and their time together feels natural again.

If neglect causes you to lose your love for each other, rest assured—you can restore it again. But why go through the difficult rebuilding process? Why not stay in love for the rest of your lives by keeping up your gift of time?

From my perspective as a marriage counselor, the time you spend alone with each other is the most valuable time of your week—and should be the most enjoyable time. It's when you are depositing the most love units and ensuring romantic love for your marriage.

Recreational Companions

When dating, it's almost effortless to make the time together enjoyable. But after marriage, if you are not careful, it can become a burden. That's because you may fail to make good adjustments to new pressures in life and to changes in the way you would like your needs met.

In every marriage, people change. What is enjoyable at twenty is often no longer fun at forty. So it's entirely possible that something both of you enjoy now will eventually become boring or even unpleasant to one of you.

Couples often make the fatal mistake of going their separate ways when an activity becomes boring to one of them. After all, they reason, why make one spouse sacrifice an enjoyable activity just to accommodate the other? If one spouse has become skilled at playing golf, for example, why give it up just because the other spouse has lost interest in the sport, especially when time and money have been invested?

The answers to those questions depend on the importance of romantic love in your marriage. If the love you have for each other is more important than your leisure activities, you should spend your most enjoyable time with each other, and that time must be mutually enjoyable.

But if your leisure activities are more important than your love, then you will pursue your favorite activities independently of each other. If that's your choice, and if you don't spend your most enjoyable time together, you will be at a high risk of losing your emotional bond and your romantic love for each other. Take my warning seriously because I've witnessed this tragic mistake thousands of times over in the lives of couples I've counseled.

One of the easiest ways to make Love Bank deposits is to enjoy leisure activities together. If you choose to spend your most enjoyable leisure time apart, however, you not only miss an opportunity to build romantic love, but someone else may make enough Love Bank deposits that you both risk having an affair.

Your love for each other should be more important than any leisure activity. That means being with each other recreationally is more important than the particular activity you choose to do together. Why? Because the most important purpose of the activity is to help build your relationship. You may want to improve your skill in that recreational activity, but that's not the primary reason you do it together.

You are not marrying each other because you enjoy playing tennis, for example. You play tennis because it's a way to be together and build your love for each other. If your spouse decides he or she doesn't enjoy tennis anymore, don't risk damaging your relationship by finding a new tennis partner. Find an alternative to tennis that will be just as enjoyable for both of you.

It's extremely important to be each other's best friend throughout life. You do that by making each other a part of every enjoyable activity you participate in. If it's fun to do, your spouse should do it with you. If your spouse doesn't enjoy doing it, try something else. Whatever activity you choose—jogging, bicycling, golfing, playing softball, or board games—be sure your spouse enjoys it, too. Don't develop skills in an activity that you can't share with your spouse.

One of the quickest ways to become bored with each other is to have more interesting things to do when you are apart. As mentioned previously, psychologists call this phenomenon the *contrast effect*—if you compare two experiences, the one that is more enjoyable will make the other seem boring. Eliminate that destructive possibility by deliberately planning your most enjoyable time to be with each other.

Spend as much of your leisure time together as possible. It is not only one of the best ways to build your relationship, but it will also help you experience the most interesting and enjoyable parts of your life together.

Spend Your Nights Together

One more word of caution for married couples: Avoid situations that keep you separated—even for one night. Separate recreational activities lead to serious marital problems because the important emotional need of recreational companionship is not being met. But when you and your partner are completely separated from each other, almost all emotional needs are not being met.

I have counseled scores of couples who began their marriage separated because one was completing an educational degree in one city while the other was beginning a new career in another city. In every case, it was a disastrous decision, one that none of them would have repeated. Even though their plan was very short-term, their failure to meet each other's emotional needs usually led to a loss of love and, in some cases, infidelity.

What about couples who choose to be separated long-term due to career paths? Instead of choosing a career that helps them meet each other's emotional needs, they choose a career that prevents it. And as would be expected, those couples experience a very high rate of divorce. The saying "If you're not with the one you love, love the one you're with" is a rule millions of unfaithful spouses use to meet their emotional needs while away from their spouse.

Early in my counseling career, I almost completely supported my family by counseling airline pilots and flight attendants, because their rate of infidelity and divorce was so high. But it isn't just those in the airline industry that suffer a high degree of marital unhappiness; it's anyone with a career that separates a couple. Long-haul truckers, traveling sales representatives, those in the military, and a host of other people with jobs that require extensive travel tend to have one thing in common: a very high rate of unfulfilling marriages, infidelity, and divorce. You can greatly lower the risk of all these disasters by simply choosing a career that encourages you to meet each other's important emotional needs almost daily.

The quality of care that a permanent romantic relationship requires is extraordinary. But it's certainly worth the effort. And it's worth the effort and the time because you'll lose your love for each other without that quality of care.

If, for some reason, your time together becomes less enjoyable, agree with each other now that you will discuss what might be going wrong and what you can do to change it. If you catch the problem early enough, while you're still in love with each other, it will be much easier to fix.

How 15 Hours Can Add Up

Joe and Sherry have full-time jobs and a 2-year-old daughter, Mary. Responsibilities with family, work, church, and friends leave them with only 2-3 hours alone each week and they are both feeling disconnected and neglected. Sherry and Joe decide to schedule more time together each week—giving each other their gift of time so they can meet each other's most important emotional needs. This is their new schedule:

Preparation:
Mary had been sleeping in their bed, so they prepared a separate sleeping place for their 2-year-old and helped her adjust to the new situation.

1. Joe's mom agreed to come over and take care of Mary once a week on Wednesday nights from 7-8:30 p.m.
2. Sherry found a babysitter who was able to work every Sunday afternoon (2-4 p.m.), during Mary's nap, and Saturday mornings (9-11 a.m.).
3. They were both exhausted by the end of the day, so they chose not to schedule undivided attention at night. Instead, they planned to go to bed 1 hour earlier and wake up 45 minutes earlier.

Plan:
1. Wake up 45 minutes earlier each weekday morning and use that time for undivided attention. (3.75 hours)
2. Talk to each other on the phone for 5 minutes every morning, noon, and afternoon during the work week. (1.25 hours)
3. Sit on the sofa when both arrive from work for undivided attention (about 15 minutes each day). (1.25 hours)
4. Every evening after Mary goes to sleep, spend 20-30 minutes together. (2.25 hours)
5. Every Saturday morning from 9-11, go out for coffee before grocery shopping together. (2 hours)
6. When Mary naps on Saturday, dedicate 1 hour for undivided attention. (1 hour)
7. Plan a recreational activity on Sunday afternoon (2-4 p.m.). (2 hours)
8. Go out for dinner on Wednesday nights, grandma babysitting (7-8:30). (1.5 hours)

Total: 15.00 hours

It's recommended that you and your partner choose a time each week to make sure you're scheduling *at least 15 hours a week together*. This schedule should include *at least 1 hour each day*. Discuss a *weekly time* with your partner (e.g., Sunday  afternoon at 3:30) where you bring your calendars and *schedule your dates for the week and times for conversation each day*. To help keep track of your time together, you may want to use *The Gift of Time* mobile app from FourGiftsofLove.org, Google Play, and Apple App Store.

Thought Questions

1. Does 15 hours seem to be an impossible goal? For some, it's challenging because they aren't used to budgeting their time. While couples budget their money so they are sure to have enough to cover their needs, they don't do the same with their time. But budgeting time is even more important. Many couples risk squandering their time if it's not budgeted—not leaving enough for their mutual happiness.

2. Still don't think it's possible? Let's do the math: You have 168 hours/week (24 hours x 7 days). If you subtract 56 hours for sleep (8 hours x 7 days), another 60 hours for work and the time it takes to commute, and 7 hours for getting up in the morning and getting ready for bed at night, that leaves you with 45 hours/week for everything else that's important. If you spend 15 hours for undivided attention with your spouse and another 15 hours caring for your children, you still have 15 hours each week for anything else that's important!

26
For the Love of Your Life

E xchanging rings at your wedding symbolize a promise. As you place the rings on each other's finger, you are making a promise to care for each other. If that promise to care means giving each other the Four Gifts of Love, then your love for each other will be guaranteed for a lifetime. Let's review these four gifts.

The Gift of Care: I promise to be your primary (human) source of happiness—to meet your most important emotional needs.

The care you promise each other is very special care—the care that lovers provide each other in a romantic relationship. It should be provided as exclusively as possible in marriage. No one else of the opposite sex should meet your needs for affection, intimate conversation, recreational companionship, and sexual fulfillment. You're likely to fall in love with the one who meets them and you want your love for each other to be exclusive.

You and your spouse are not likely to prioritize the intimate emotional needs in the same order of importance. Sexual fulfillment and recreational companionship are likely to be more important to a husband, and affection and intimate conversation are likely to be more important to a wife. To fulfill your promise  to care for each other, you will probably be meeting needs that do not seem important to you as they are to your spouse. He or she will depend on you to meet those needs.

In addition to the four emotional needs just mentioned, there are others that you will be expecting each other to meet. Be sure that you have identified them for each other and place them in order of their importance to you. Your promise to meet those needs will define the way you will be caring for each other throughout your life together.

The Gift of Protection: I promise to avoid being a source of your unhappiness—to avoid Love Busters.

When you give the gift of care, you become the greatest source of each other's happiness. But you can also become the greatest source of each other's unhappiness unless you do something to prevent it. That's why the gift of protection is equally important.

 You and your partner were both born to be demanding, disrespectful, angry, dishonest, annoying, and independent. I call these human traits Love Busters because they destroy the feeling of love couples have for each other. But if you promise to avoid being the cause of your partner's unhappiness, you will do whatever it takes to overcome these destructive tendencies for his or her protection. By eliminating Love Busters, you will not only be protecting your partner, but you will also be preserving your partner's love for you.

Almost everything you do will affect each other, so it's very important to know what the effect will be before you do anything. And it's especially important to know the effect when you make lifestyle decisions. After all, the life you will be creating together should make both of you happy.

The Policy of Joint Agreement will help you remember to avoid being the cause of each other's unhappiness. It will remind you to consider each other's feelings and interests throughout your lives. By making mutually acceptable choices, you will create a lifestyle that you will both enjoy, rather than creating one that benefits one of you at the expense of the other.

The Gift of Honesty: I promise to be transparent with you.

Your promise to be honest requires you to be transparent to each other. You should be honest about your feelings, personal history, current activities and experiences, and future plans. It is *complete* honesty.

It won't be easy for you to keep your promise to be honest. As I already mentioned, we're born to be dishonest. Honesty requires effort. And it's an unpopular value these days. Most couples view personal privacy to be more important than honesty. In fact, some marriage counselors and clergy argue that honesty is  not the best policy: They believe that it's cruel and selfish to disclose past indiscretions. Some believe that the primary reason spouses are honest about mistakes of the past is to feel better, to get these little demons off their chest. Since such revelations cause a partner to feel bad, they argue, the truly caring thing is to lie about your mistakes or at least keep them tucked away.

If it's compassionate to lie about the mistakes of the past, why isn't it also compassionate to lie about mistakes of the present or future? To my way of thinking, it's like letting the proverbial camel's nose into the tent. Eventually, you will be dining with the camel. Either honesty is always right, or you'll always have an excuse for being dishonest.

Self-imposed honesty with your partner is essential to your marriage's safety and success. Honesty will not only bring you closer to each other emotionally, but it will also prevent the creation of destructive habits that are kept secret from your partner. The Policy of Radical Honesty combined with the Policy of

Joint Agreement will assist you in creating an open and integrated lifestyle, one that will help guarantee your love for each other.

The Gift of Time: I promise to follow the Policy of Undivided Attention.

The gift of time unlocks the door to the three other gifts. Without it, you will not be able to meet each other's emotional needs, nor will you be able to avoid being the cause of each other's unhappiness. Time is also a basic requirement for honesty. Time for undivided attention is the necessary ingredient for everything important in your marriage.

But as soon as a couple is married, and especially when children arrive, they are tempted to replace their time together with activities of lesser importance. They try to meet each other's needs with time "leftover," but sadly there won't be any. Their lack of private time together will become a great cause of frustration, yet they feel incapable of preventing it. They also find themselves bottling up their honest expression of feelings because there is just no appropriate time to talk.

The solution to this problem is to schedule a minimum of fifteen hours each week to be alone with each other. And that time should be used to meet each other's most important emotional needs—affection, intimate conversation, recreational companionship, and sexual fulfillment. Make it your highest priority and then it will never be replaced by anything of lesser value. Your career, time with your children, maintenance of your home, and a host of other demands will all compete for your time together. But if you promise each other the gift of time, you will not let anything steal from you those precious hours together.

Putting It All Together

Why would you want to continue creating a lifestyle that gives these Gifts of Love to your spouse and God? Answer: This lifestyle sustains passion for God and the feeling of romantic love in marriage.

Why would you want to sustain your passion for God and the feeling of romantic love in marriage? Answer: We can have a marriage without romantic love and a relationship with God that lacks passion, but it doesn't have to be that way. By creating a lifestyle that gives and receives the Four Gifts of Love, those relationships can be filled with incredible feelings.

Those feelings are a result of a lifestyle of care, protection, honesty, and time. Those feelings bring increased joy in life. And those feelings make it *easier* to care, protect, be honest, and give time with those feelings.

If you lose those feelings, it takes energy and willpower to re-create the lifestyle that will restore them. And as you reviewed in chapter One, these are two relationships that impact your life the most!

Why do this? Simple answer...It's WORTH it! And it's what God intended from the beginning of our creation (Genesis 1 and 2).

Four Gifts: The Foundation for a Lifetime of Love

We have devoted our lives to helping couples create successful marriages. They achieve that objective by giving each other the four gifts we've discussed in this workbook. These promises have allowed millions of couples to avoid marital tragedy and to create a lifetime of love.

Marriage can be terrific for every couple that follows these simple rules. But most begin their marriage without knowing how to make Love Bank deposits and to avoid withdrawals. They think that the love they feel for each other on their wedding day will carry them through life, regardless of the way they treat each other. Most of them don't realize that without care, protection, honesty, and time they will lose that love, and along with it, a fulfilling marriage.

You have the recipe to help you create what very few couples ever achieve—love that lasts a lifetime. And your love for each other is not all you will achieve. You will find that with these four gifts, your children will be happier and more successful, your careers will flourish, you will be healthier, and your outlook on life will be optimistic and confident. There are so many advantages to these four gifts that they should be your highest priority.

We wish you a happy and fulfilling marriage. And these four gifts can make it possible.

Talk About This

1. How many hours during the three-day period did you spend giving God the gift of time? _____ Divide that number by 3 to get a daily average: _____ hours/day. Is this average daily time with God typical for you? Does this amount meet your goal?

2. What are some ideas for increasing that time with God? Specifically, during what time of the day can you add more time?

3. How many hours during the three-day period did you spend giving your partner the gift of time? _____ Divide that number by 3 to get a daily average: _____ hours/day. Is this amount of time with your partner typical for you? Does this amount meet your goal?

4. What are some ideas for increasing that time with your partner? Specifically, during what time of the day can you add more time? (Reminder: To help keep track of your time

together, you can use *The Gift of Time* mobile app from FourGiftsofLove.org, Google Play, and Apple App Store.)

5. If you were to lose your feeling of love for an innocent reason (being separated for a while due to circumstances beyond your control), would you also tend to lose your willingness to care for each other? That can happen in marriage and it creates what psychologists call a negative feedback loop: The less you love each other, the less you feel like caring, which then causes you to love each other less. What would you feel like doing if your feeling of love for each other were to slip a notch? What should you do to rebuild your Love Bank balances?

27
Parting Words

The purpose of creating this material that represents over 70 years of our cumulative experience was for you to have a terrific relationship with your partner and with God. But there's more! Most couples that seek our professional help do not come wanting to build a stronger marriage from an already satisfying relationship. Instead, most come with their marriage in near ruin—victims of infidelity, mental and physical abuse, and emotional abandonment. If I received a coin for each time a client told me, *I wish we had followed the Four Gifts of Love years ago,* I'd definitely have a large piggy bank full of coins.

When couples create a lifestyle that fails to provide the Four Gifts of Love to a spouse and to God, the result is disastrous. And our years of experience prove that fact. Day after day, we hear the tragic stories of those who have followed that sad path.

It's these experiences, and our love for Christ, that inspired us to write this curriculum as a gift to you. Our heart's desire is for you to look forward to a wonderful life together and be spared the suffering that so many couples experience. And our wish for you has been a proven reality for thousands who have given and received these Four Gifts of Love to their spouse and to God.

So as you approach your wedding day or continue your life as husband and wife, let us leave you with some parting words of advice:

> Make the Four Gifts of Love your life's template.

- You will have choice points in your life—when to have a child, what job to take, where to move, what budget to follow, what to do this weekend, whether or not to join a sports team, etc. With every decision, make it your goal to keep romantic love in your marriage and to keep a God-glorifying lifestyle. Make the Four Gifts of Love your life's template. For example, if you are thinking about a particular job, ask yourselves, *Will we be able to maintain our daily time together? Will we be able to care for each other? Will we be able to maintain an honest relationship? Will we be able to maintain a caring relationship with God?* By following this template, many tragic outcomes can be avoided.

- Bells and whistles don't sound off when you have taken a path that leads to tragedy. That's why we recommend keeping a regularly scheduled review throughout your marriage. Have you marked your calendar—the 1st of every month for the next year (or set cell phone alarms)? Use this review to receive feedback and remind yourself of these gifts given to your spouse and God. It's easy to get out of thoughtful habits and into thoughtless ones. You will need continual reminders to stay on track. And a habit of reviewing the Four Gifts of Love will allow you to make critical lifestyle adjustments *before* troubles arise.

- **Protect your Love Bank**. Falling in love with someone other than your spouse is easier than you think. As a matter of fact, you're wired to have an affair, and most marriages suffer the tragic consequences! It starts innocently by regularly allowing someone to meet your most important emotional needs (e.g., talking together, showing acts of kindness, sharing a recreational activity). If you give someone of the opposite gender time to meet your most important emotional needs, they will make Love Bank deposits. And the greater the Love Bank account becomes, the more difficult it is to resist an affair. Here are some possible rules to help guard your Love Bank:

1. Avoid meeting the most important emotional needs, and having those met, by someone of the opposite sex other than your spouse, with special emphasis on affection, sexual fulfillment, intimate conversation, recreational companionship, and admiration.

2. Avoid contact with those you once loved. Parenting issues with an ex-spouse should be managed by your spouse.

3. If you ever find yourself infatuated with someone other than your spouse, for whatever reasons, don't walk away—run! And tell your spouse.

4. If someone tells you that he or she finds you attractive, be prepared to tell how much you love your spouse. Then tell your spouse.

5. If your spouse's job or your job requires travel, use additional precautions to avoid increased vulnerability and opportunity (e.g., limit anything that would lower your inhibitions, like alcohol).

These are simply thoughtful rules that give your spouse the gifts of protection and honesty—helping you avoid a common tragedy.

• **Caring for your spouse is a way to worship God**. God has assigned an important job to you—meeting certain emotional needs for your spouse. The way you meet those needs and show your spouse care is a way of showing honor to God. The care you show each other in marriage is very important to God. In fact, marriage is cited in Scripture as an analogy of the love God has for us (Ephesians 5:25). It's a sacred relationship instituted by God

(Genesis 2:24; Matthew 19:4-6). Remember this fact as you live each day giving your spouse the gift of care, protection, honesty, and time.

- **We aren't perfect.** This isn't a major revelation—we all know that there are days that we don't do what we promise to do. And you and your partner won't give each other the Four Gifts of Love exactly as promised either. You'll occasionally make a thoughtless decision, you'll let something interfere with your time together, or you'll blurt out a disrespectful judgment. And there will also be days when you fail to fulfill your promises to God. You'll fail to make His will a part of each decision you make, or you'll do something harmful to someone He loves. The scheduled reviews mentioned above should keep you from straying too far off the Four Gifts of Love path. But when this happens, you will need to learn how to "re-up." It's a military term that means "to re-enlist for service." If you start to stray from the path, be prepared to "re-up" or re-enlist to fulfill your promises to God and your partner. A commitment to "re-up" will help keep you giving and receiving these gifts of love.

Action Step: Your parting action step is to complete the **Marital Promise.** You may sign it now, after your marriage ceremony, during your ceremony, or on a special date. This is a gift to each other that will protect your love for a lifetime. As you sign your marital promise, also make another promise by signing the **Promise to God**—to continue giving Him your gifts of love and accepting His on a daily basis. This is a gift that will protect your feelings of excitement for God and keep your eyes on pleasing Him.

A fillable pdf for each promise is available at https://www.FourGiftsofLove.Org (resources/questionnaires).

And, if you would like a review of the readings in this book and concepts, and receive in-depth guidance and encouragement for the action steps, please consider taking the Four Gifts of Love® Class (https://www.FourGiftsofLove.Org/four-gifts-of-love-class or scan the QR code).

This interactive and multimedia approach to marriage/pre-marriage education encourages couples to create a lifestyle that will help sustain the feeling of romantic love for a lifetime and sustain a passion for God. Based upon the time-tested marriage concepts of Dr. Willard F. Harley, Jr., an internationally-known author of over 20 marriage books, including *His Needs, Her Needs* (Harley, 1986, 2022) with over 23 translations, this empirically-based class utilizes professionally animated and acted videos, engaging questions, questionnaires, reading material, and much more!

Marital Promise

This Agreement is made the _____ day of _____, 20_____, between _____, hereinafter called "husband," and _____, hereinafter called "wife," whereby it is mutually agreed:

I. The husband and wife agree to give the **Gift of Protection**—to avoid being a source of your spouse's unhappiness.

    A. To avoid making thoughtless decisions, the husband and wife agree to follow the Policy of Joint Agreement—Never do anything without an enthusiastic agreement between you and your spouse. This policy guarantees that one spouse will not gain at the other's expense.

    B. To avoid thoughtless behavior, the husband and wife agree to protect each other from the following Love Busters:

        1. Angry Outbursts: Deliberate attempts to hurt the other because of anger, usually in the form of verbal or physical attacks. If angry outbursts occur, the husband and wife will follow a course of action that identifies angry outbursts, investigates their motives and causes, keeps a record of their occurrences and eliminates them.

        2. Disrespectful Judgments: Attempts to change the other's attitudes, beliefs, and behavior by trying to force his/her way of thinking through lecture, ridicule, threat, or other means. If disrespectful judgments occur, the husband and wife will follow a course of action that identifies disrespectful judgments, investigates their

causes, keeps a record of their occurrences and eliminates the behavior.

3. Annoying Habits: Habits that cause the other to be unhappy. If annoying behavior occurs, the husband and wife will follow the course of action that identifies annoying behavior, investigates the motives and causes of the behavior, keeps a record of their occurrences and eliminates the behavior.

4. Selfish Demands: Attempts to force the other to do something with implied threat of punishment if he or she refuses. If selfish demands occur, the husband and wife will follow a course of action that identifies selfish demands, investigates their causes, keeps a record of their occurrences and replaces them with thoughtful requests.

5. Independent Behavior: Behavior conceived and executed by your spouse without consideration of your feelings. These behaviors are usually scheduled and require thought to complete, such as attending sporting events or engaging in a personal exercise program.

6. Dishonesty: Failure to reveal to the other correct information about emotional reactions, personal history, daily activities, and plans for the future. If dishonesty occurs, the husband and wife will follow a course of action that identifies dishonesty, investigates its causes, records its occurrence, and replaces it with emotional, historical, current, future, and complete honesty.

II. The husband and wife agree to follow the **Gift of Care**—to be a primary source of happiness by meeting your spouse's most important emotional needs. They will do this by:

A. The husband and wife will give the Gift of Care by identifying each other's emotional needs and selecting at least five that are most important to the husband and at least five that are most important to the wife. Those needs may include the following:

1. Affection: To receive nonsexual expressions of care symbolizing security, protection, and comfort, which may include words, cards, gifts, hugs, kisses, and courtesies from the husband/wife.

2. Sexual Fulfillment: To engage in an enjoyable sexual experience with the husband/wife.

3. Intimate Conversation: To share feelings, personal experiences, topics of personal interest, opinions, and plans with the husband/wife.

4. Recreational Companionship: To engage in recreational activities with the husband/wife.

5. Honesty and Openness: To receive truthful and frank information from the husband/wife about positive and negative feelings, events of the past, daily events and schedule, and plans for the future.

6. Physical Attractiveness: To observe the husband's/wife's physical appearance that the spouse finds aesthetically and/or sexually pleasing.

7. Financial Support: To receive help from the husband/wife with financial resources to house, feed, and clothe the family.

8. Domestic Support: To receive help from the husband/wife with household tasks and care of the children (if any are at home).

9. Family Commitment: To receive help from the husband/wife with the moral and educational development of the children within the family unit.

10. Admiration: To be shown respect, value, and appreciation by the husband/wife.

The husband's five most important emotional needs ranked in order are:

1) _____

2) _____

3) _____

4) _____

5) _____

The wife's five most important emotional needs ranked in order are:

1) _____

2) _____

3) _____

4) _____

5) _____

B. The husband and wife will give the Gift of Care by creating plans to help form new habits that will meet their spouse's five needs.

C. The husband and wife will give the Gift of Care by evaluating the success of their plans, creating new plans if the first are unsuccessful; learning to meet new marital needs if their spouse replaces any of the original five with new needs.

They will meet every _____ (week, month, quarter, year) to review this agreement and change it, if needed.

III. The husband and wife agree to the **Gift of Time**—Take time to give your spouse undivided attention, using the time to provide the most meaningful acts of care for the other. They will do this by:

A. Ensuring privacy, planning time together that does not include children, relatives, or friends so that undivided attention is maximized.

B. Using the time to meet the needs of affection, sexual fulfillment, conversation, and recreational companionship.

C. Choosing a number of hours that reflects the quality of marriage: Fifteen hours each week if the marriage is mutually satisfying, and more time if marital dissatisfaction is reported by either spouse.

D. Scheduling time to be together prior to each week and keeping a permanent record of the time actually spent.

IV. The husband and wife agree to the **Gift of Honesty**—Be completely open and honest with your spouse. They will do this by being:

A. Emotionally Honest: Revealing to each other their emotional reactions--both positive and negative—to the events of their lives, particularly each other's behavior.

B. Historically Honest: Revealing information about their personal histories, particularly events that demonstrate personal weaknesses or failure.

C. Currently Honest: Revealing information about the events of their day, providing each other with a calendar of their activities, with special emphasis on those that may affect each other.

D. Honest about the Future: Revealing their thoughts and plans regarding future activities and objectives.

E. Completely Honest: Not leaving each other with a false impression regarding their thoughts, feelings, habits, likes, dislikes, personal history, daily activities or plans for the future. They will not keep any personal information from each other.

IN WITNESS WHEREOF, the parties hereto have signed this agreement on the day and year first above written:

_____

Husband

_____

Wife

_____

Witness (optional)

Marital Promise Summary

My marital promises are about

EXTRAORDINARY care for you.

I Promise to give you the **gift of care**: to be a source of happiness.

- Developing skills and habits to meet your most important emotional needs
- Being honest with you about mutuality
- Reviewing my plan of care with you at least every year

I Promise to give you the **gift of protection**: to avoid being a source of unhappiness.

- Developing skills to avoid my Love Busters and create alternative habits
- Valuing your honesty
- Making decisions with mutual enthusiastic agreement
- Reviewing my plan of protection with you at least every year

I Promise to give you the **gift of honesty**: to be completely open and honest.

- Using specific, positive alternative suggestions about my desires
- Giving my complete, transparent honesty
- Avoiding Love Busters when being honest

I Promise to give you the **gift of time**: to give undivided attention, using the time to meet your most important emotional needs.

- Scheduling 15 hours each week for private, undivided attention
- Using the time to meet our intimate emotional needs

Promise to God

THIS PLEDGE is made this _____ day of _____,
20_____.

I PROMISE to continue developing and implementing my plans to:
1. Respect and honor You
2. Love You through continuing fellowship
3. Love others with Your attitude of love and meaningful acts of care
4. Tell non-Christians about my faith in Jesus Christ
5. Continue to grow in my understanding of You

I PROMISE to use the four steps of problem-solving to ensure that I:
1. Come to You in prayer regarding my problems
2. Have faith, that with Your help, the problem can be solved
3. Think of ways the problem could be solved
4. Implement a plan to solve the problem

I PROMISE to schedule daily time with you where I praise You, confess the sinful behavior that I've done and commit to a plan of change, give You thanks, and tell You my concerns and desires of my heart.

I PROMISE to review my Four Gifts of Love® plan on the first of every month so I will sustain a lifestyle that gives You my gifts of love.

I PROMISE to include You in every decision I make.

IN WITNESS WHEREOF, I sign this agreement, not only on paper but, most importantly, within my heart.

_____
My Signature

_____
Witness to My Pledge

About the Authors

Jennifer Harley Chalmers, Ph.D., and Willard F. Harley, Jr., Ph.D., her father, are licensed psychologists and marriage counselors. For over 25 years they have collaborated to create and improve methods that restore love to marriages. Their primary effort has focused on the recovery of marriage following an affair (*Surviving an Affair*, Harley/Chalmers, 1998, 2013).

Dr. Harley's innovative marriage counseling methods are described in his numerous books and articles he writes. *His Needs, Her Needs: Building an Affair-proof Marriage* has been a best-seller since it was published in 1986 and has been translated into over 22 foreign languages. He and Joyce, his wife of over 60 years, also offer a daily radio program called Marriage Builders® Radio (available by Mobile App). Their son, Steve, is also a marriage counselor, and the administrator and co-developer of the internationally-known MarriageBuilders.com website.

Dr. Chalmers is also an international speaker, author, and administrator and developer of the **FourGiftsofLove.Org**, **FourGiftsofLove.Com** and **Foundation4Marriage.Com** websites. She and Phil, her husband of over 38 years, teach Four Gifts of Love® Classes together. They have two adult daughters and a son-in-law and live in the Philippines and Minnesota, USA.

Please visit our website for many free marriage resources (videos, articles, online classes, mobile apps, and much more). For your convenience, here is a QR code for the FourGiftsofLove.org site:

Resources by the Authors

- ***Let's Get Growing, Christians!*** (Harley/ Chalmers, 2003) provides a practical guide for Christians who want to create a lifestyle of doing God's will. This book also provides a group format.

- ***Draw Close*** (Harley/Harley, 2011) is a devotional that helps you connect with your spouse, build a stronger marriage, and keep God at the center of your commitment to each other.

- ***Surviving an Affair*** (Harley/Chalmers, 1998, 2013) provides answers to those who find themselves caught in the common tragedy of infidelity. From the moment an affair is first suspected all the way through full marital recovery, this book provides a thorough analysis and step-by-step proven solutions. It's written especially for the betrayed spouse, but has invaluable guidance for everyone involved.

- ***His Needs, Her Needs*** (Harley, 1986, 2022) helps couples learn to identify and meet each other's most important emotional needs. This classic marriage guide has been translated in over 22 different languages, with over 5 million in print.

- ***His Needs, Her Needs for Parents*** (Harley, 2003, 2017) is a guide to why and how to keep your marriage healthy. It offers specific, practical steps on meeting each other's needs and giving your kids what they need by putting your spouse first. You can maintain your love for each other, and raise happy and successful children at the same time...this book points the way.

- *Love Busters: Overcoming Habits that Destroy Romantic Love* (Harley, 1992, 1997, 2002, 2008, 2016) helps couples learn to avoid being the cause of each other's unhappiness.

- *Five Steps to Romantic Love* (Harley, 1993, 2002) is a workbook to help couples apply the principles found in *His Needs, Her Needs* and *Love Busters.* The contracts, questionnaires, inventories and worksheets that Dr. Harley has used in his counseling practice are arranged in a logical sequence to help couples follow Dr. Harley's Five Steps: (1) make a commitment to overcome marital problems, (2) identify habits that cause unhappiness, (3) learn to overcome those habits, (4) identify the most important emotional needs, and (5) learn to meet those needs.

- *He Wins, She Wins: Learning the Art of Marital Negotiation* (Harley, 2013) gets to the heart of marital conflicts and offers a time-tested way to resolve them. Then he walks you through the five most common sources of conflict in marriage and how to overcome obstacles to resolve conflicts.

- *He Wins, She Wins Workbook* (Harley, 2015) is a practical workbook that walks couples through scenarios for the five most common areas of conflict in marriage—friends and family, career and time management, finances, raising children, and sex—applying the Policy of Joint Agreement in every situation. Couples practice resolving each of these conflicts the right way, before turning attention to their own real-life conflicts.

- *Fall in Love, Stay in Love* (Harley, 2001) weaves together the insights and techniques Dr. Harley has collected over the years into a comprehensive plan for building and sustaining the feeling of love. In seventeen sessions it equips you with the tools you need for a happy, successful marriage.

- *The One: Buyers, Renters, and Freeloaders* (Harley, 2002) helps singles turn revolving-door romance into lasting love. It provides a tried and proven plan for building a long-term relationship.

Mobile App Resource/Website:

To refresh your understanding of the FGL concepts, visit **https://www.FourGiftsofLove.org** for online courses and **Mobile Apps**: **E^2: Engage and Explore, Gift of Care, Gift of Protection, Gift of Honesty, Gift of Time**, **Let's Negotiate**, and **WHY?** Scan the QR code to view the mobile apps.

WANT TO LEARN MORE?

Now that you have read *Foundation 4 Marriage*, we recommend that you consider taking the Four Gifts of Love® Class. This eight-lesson class offers a review of the readings within this book, but also provides professionally-animated review videos, more in-depth guided assignments, questionnaires, and much more. This class provides a bridge from knowledge to a Four Gifts of Love® lifestyle. Please visit **https://www.FourGiftsofLove.Org** for  more information about starting your first lesson for free (online format) or scan the QR code.